Bavaria

Written and Presented by **Anne Midgette**

Anne Midgette

INSIGHT
Pocket
GUIDES

Insight Pocket Guide:

BAVARIA

Directed by
Hans Höfer

Managing Editor
Tony Halliday

Photography by
Marton Radkai and others

Design Concept by
V. Barl

Design by
Carlotta Junger

© 1993 APA Publications (HK) Ltd

All Rights Reserved

Printed in Singapore by
Höfer Press (Pte) Ltd
Fax: 65-8616438

Distributed in the UK & Ireland by
GeoCenter International UK Ltd
The Viables Center, Harrow Way
Basingstoke, Hampshire RG22 4BJ
ISBN: 9-62421-576-6

Worldwide distribution enquiries:
Höfer Communications Pte Ltd
38 Joo Koon Road
Singapore 2262
ISBN: 9-62421-576-6

Welcome! I'll never forget my first view of the 'real Bavaria'. Three days after I'd arrived from the States back in the summer of 1986, some friends loaded me into their car and whisked me off to a grassy meadow nestling among wooded hills on the deep blue sides of snowcapped Alps. In a striped tent people were drinking mugs of beer at long wooden tables while green-clad men with what looked like shaving brushes on their hats oom-pahed away on brass instruments. I looked up through the open end of the tent and saw, just behind us, the spires of a fairy-tale castle on the nearest height: it was Mad King Ludwig's famous Neuschwanstein. At that moment, I wondered if I'd left reality altogether.

Since then, I've been living and working as a journalist in Munich, and have come to realise that Bavaria is very much a country unto itself. The image many foreigners have of a 'typical' German is actually a Bavarian, sporting *Lederhosen* and quaffing a huge mug of beer. This image represents only the most obvious elements of a deeply established, centuries-old folk culture. Those *Lederhosen* are a part of the elaborate, traditional *Tracht* (folk costumes), which are different for every village; that beer has been brewed to conform with the strict purity laws enacted in the 16th century, from a tradition born in monastic breweries. And if you can't understand what your typical Bavarian is saying, don't worry: most other Germans also have problems with the distinctive local dialect.

Bavarians are proud of their culture, and are as eager to remain distinct from the northern Germans as the northern Germans, jealous, perhaps, of the long and established Bavarian history, are to keep their distance from their quirky neighbours to the south. 'Why do they call it the Free State of Bavaria?' runs one German joke. 'Because it's the only place in the world where they let the Bavarians run around free'.

Welcome – Grüß Gott! — Anne Midgette

CONTENTS

Preceding pages:
a fairy-tale land.

Following pages:
the festive spirit

Bavaria's borders have fluctuated over the centuries, but its core has remained fundamentally unchanged; the land between the river Danube and the Alps, the rivers Lech and Inn, has consistently remained the centre of a single political, sociological entity.

The first 'Bavarians' lived here about 600,000 years ago, but the Celts, who appeared between 700 and 500BC, made a far more tangible mark on the region. Their legacies include the remains of villages and religious sites as well as some blond-haired, blue-eyed genes which crop up now and then among the generally dark-complexioned locals.

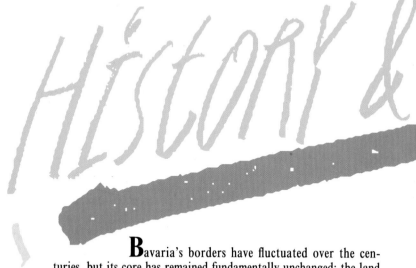

In 15BC, Augustus Caesar's Roman armies marched in and conquered all of Southern Germany in a single summer. In their new province, *Rhaetium*, the ever-efficient Romans set up military encampments, many of which became urban centres that still exist today. One such is *Rhaetium's* capital *Augusta Vindelicum*, today known as Augsburg; there are other Roman remains in *Castra Regina* (Regensburg) and *Boiodurum* (Passau).

But Rome gradually overextended itself until Imperial troops could no longer withstand the onslaughts of Germanic tribes – at home or abroad. In AD476, Odoacer, leader of Germanic troops within the Roman armies, overthrew the Roman Emperor, establishing an Ostrogoth Empire and ending the Roman Empire for good.

Mask of a Roman soldier

Culture

Early Christians and Medieval Dukes

When the Romans were gone, so popular legend has it, the *Baiuvarii* tribe returned to the lands from which they'd been expelled. During the reign of the Agilolfing family in the 7th century, Irish monks zealously embarked on missionary work. Saints and martyrs Magnus, Boniface, and Kilian were among those who spread the Catholic gospels and established bishoprics, churches and monasteries (the Marienkapelle in Würzburg, St Emmeram in Regensburg, and Benedictine monasteries on Lake Chiemsee).

Selling spices

In 788, Charlemagne decided that Duke Tassilo III of the Agilofing family was getting too big for his britches, deposed him, and absorbed his territories into the Carolingian Empire. The Carolingian dynasty died out, however, in 911, and control of the region was hotly disputed over the next two centuries. Significant among the six dynasties who held power during this period were the Welfs, whose rule saw the growth of a little river community called Munichen (München, or Munich); but Emperor Frederick I Barbarossa, tired of their frequent bids for more power, got rid of them in 1180, awarding the duchy to Otto I of the house of Wittelsbach. It was an auspicious move: the Wittelsbachs ruled in Bavaria as Dukes, Electors, and finally Kings, for 738 years.

The first Wittelsbach rulers devoted themselves to the pursuit of new territory, and were so successful that they were among the Holy Roman Empire's most important ruling dynasties by the middle of the 13th century. Arguments over succession, however, divided the duchy and undermined its power. The one truly strong ruler during the 14th and 15th centuries was Ludwig the Bavarian (who had himself crowned Emperor in 1327), but the power and

Jakob Fugger's office

land gain he achieved was rapidly forgotten in territorial disputes between his six sons after his death.

Fortunately, political turmoil did not affect the art and architecture of the period. Romanesque churches made way for the soaring Gothic cathedrals of Regensburg, Munich, Landshut and Rothenburg. On the literary front, the *Nibelung* epic was completed in Passau around 1200, while, in Landshut, Wolfram von Eschenbach was finishing his poem *Parzifal* (both works later became the basis for operas by 19th-century composer Richard Wagner). And the political insignificance of Bavaria's ruling families was balanced by the increasing power of private citizens such as the Fuggers of Augsburg, whose patriarch Jakob used his fortune to influence Imperial elections in 1519. Most Bavarians, however, lived as farmers in the countryside. Apart from the profitable salt trade there was little industry.

Bavaria Reunited

Duke Albrecht IV was tired of seeing Bavaria subdivided – and he didn't want to share the task of governing with his brother. In 1506, he established the principle of primogeniture, whereby only firstborn sons should govern; Bavaria remained under the control of one ruler until the end of the Wittelsbach era.

It was the dawn of the Renaissance. Tilman Riemenschneider and Veit Stoss were carving magnificent altars and figures for churches throughout Bavaria; Riemenschneider even had the temerity to enter politics, becoming Mayor of Würzburg in 1520. Equal skill was shown by Bavarian painters Lucas Cranach, Hans Holbein father and son, and Nuremberg native Albrecht Dürer, whose self-portraits were not only some of the finest of the Renaissance, but some of the first.

Martin Luther, meanwhile, was making waves with radical clerical reforms which split Europe into two bitterly warring factions, Catholic and Protestant. Although a German, Luther found little support in Catholic Bavaria; leaders such as Wilhelm the Pious ensured that the state remained a centre for the Counter-Reformation. Some neigh-

Wood-carving by Veit Stoss

bouring, at that time non-Bavarian, cities such as Nuremberg and Regensburg did vote to become Protestant, however, sowing the seeds of divisiveness in the region.

When Duke Maximilian I took power in 1597, Bavaria was riddled with debt after the rules of two spendthrift dukes. Maximilian, however, was equal to the challenge; a born leader who was famously industrious (starting work each morning before 5am), he brought the state's account books solidly into the black within 12 years. He didn't only prove his mettle on the home front: founder of the defensive Catholic League in 1609, he led its troops to victory in the Thirty Years' War. His success was crowned when the grateful Emperor elevated him from Duke to Elector (*Kurfürst*) in 1623. Ironically, this war, which hit Bavaria hard (900 cities and towns were destroyed, and half the population lost), also helped to establish the state's importance on the European political scene. Maximilian ruled throughout the war; he died in 1651.

Maximilian I

The physical devastation of the Thirty Years' War did have some positive consequences: people began building like mad to replace what had been lost. As new churches, palaces and administrative buildings sprang up, so did a style which was to become a hallmark of the region: Bavarian baroque. Imported from Italy by Elector Ferdinand Maria's Turin-born wife Henriette Adelaide in 1663 when she commissioned the Theatiner Church in Munich, the new style spread like wildfire, soon producing German artists able to equal, even surpass, their Italian models. Among these were the Asam brothers, Egid Quirin and Cosmas Damian, and Balthasar Neumann, who designed the Würzburg Residenz. And the word *barockisiert*, 'baroque-ised', was added to the German vocabulary as old buildings throughout Bavaria were redone in the new fashion.

Leaders and Ladies

In the late 1700s, Bavaria's political scene was dominated by one of the country's most ingenious politicians: Elector Max IV Joseph's Foreign Minister, Count Montgelas. Forced to choose between France and Austria as Europe prepared itself for yet another war, both Elector and Minister opted for France and Napoleon, signing a treaty of alliance in 1805. The decision was opportune: Napoleon promptly trounced Austria and rewarded Bavaria's loyalty with large land grants (including Augsburg and Passau) and the official title of Kingdom.

Francophilia, however, waned soon enough; in 1813, the pragmatic Bavarians switched sides. Their new treaty with Austria

placed them on the side of the victorious powers at the 1815 Congress of Vienna after Napoleon's final defeat. At the Congress, new territorial grants gave Bavaria approximately the shape it has today.

Bavaria's next ruler was King Ludwig I, who filled Munich with new museums and cultural institutions, like the Alte and Neue Pinakothek, designed by royal favourite Leo von Klenze. Besides architecture, Ludwig's consuming passion was women: a series of portraits he commissioned of the kingdom's 'most beautiful women' fills an entire room in Nymphenburg Palace. This weakness for the ladies brought about the King's downfall. When 'Spanish' dancer Lola Montez (actually an Irishwoman from Limerick) performed in the National Theatre, King Ludwig was immediately smitten. His blatant attachment fuelled rising animosity among the population; ultimately, a revolution in the stormy year of 1848 forced Ludwig to abdicate in favour of his son, Maximilian II.

Dreams and Reality

In 1864, Maximilian's death cleared the throne for one of the most fantastic characters in Bavaria's history: his son, King Ludwig II. The young king, a daydreamer and passionate builder, spent all of the kingdom's money constructing castles which seemed as unusual to his contemporaries as they do today, such as the famous Neuschwanstein. Politically, the most significant act of Ludwig's reign was Bavaria's entry into the new, Prussian-led German Empire, proclaimed in 1871. For the first time in centuries, Bavaria was in a submissive position among German states.

The young Ludwig II

Ludwig's eccentric behaviour became more and more pronounced, and in 1886, he was officially diagnosed as insane. A week later, he was found with his doctor, drowned; one of the region's favourite unsolved mysteries is the question of whether it was suicide or murder. Although he bled his country's coffers dry, 'Mad' King Ludwig remained fixed in the popular imagination, and to this day his portrait graces shops and homes throughout Bavaria.

As Ludwig's brother Otto was even crazier than his sibling, 65-year-old Uncle Luitpold stepped in

Kurt Eisner proclaimed Bavaria a Republic

as Prince Regent, ruling until his death at the grand old age of 91. After the flighty control of Ludwig II, who had been happy to leave the work of governing to his ministers, Luitpold brought dignity back to the monarchy without undermining the power of the parliaments, and returned prosperity and solidity to the land. After Luitpold's death, his son put an end to the regency and ascended the throne as King Ludwig III.

When the German Empire declared a state of war in 1914, Bavaria had little choice but to go along with it – and little inclination to do anything else. With the rest of the German states, the region mobilised and sent troops out to fight the bloody battles of World War I. As German losses mounted, however, unrest began at home, leading, in Bavaria, to revolution. In 1918, socialist leader Kurt Eisner proclaimed Bavaria a Free People's Republic, and announced that Wittelsbach rule was at an end. The ensuing tumultuous months saw the assassination of Eisner, the establishment of a soviet republic, or *Räterepublik*, and its violent overthrow at the hands of the conservative White Guard.

The storm died down when the 'Bamberg Constitution' officially termed Bavaria a 'Free State and Member of the German Empire'; but this did nothing to solve unemployment and inflation so extreme that it took an entire wheelbarrow full of money to buy a loaf of bread. Suffering from privation and angry at ineffective leadership, the people were looking for a saviour; and they saw him in an Austrian named Adolf Hitler. Although Hitler's first bid for power in a Munich beer hall in 1923 was put down, his National Socialist party continued to gain ground; in 1933, he was named Chancellor and the Third Reich had begun.

Hitler was indeed able to bolster the economy; but he also dreamed of restoring to Germany the boundaries of the Holy Roman Empire, while clearing it of 'undesirables' such as Jews and homosexuals, whom he exterminated in concentration camps. 1939 saw the invasion of Poland, the beginning of the Nazi march across Europe. When the tide began to turn in the Allies' favour, retribution came in the form of massive bombings of virtually every major German city. In 1945, after the final Nazi defeat, cities like Munich, Würzburg, Augsburg and Nuremberg were literally levelled, with only fragments of walls rising from the rubble.

Resistance leaders Hans and Sophie Scholl

Modernity and Tradition

Germany's rehabilitation in the eyes of the world has proceeded at varying speeds. The 1950s 'economic miracle' (*Wirtschaftswunder*), when the country was rebuilt and became prosperous in the space of a decade, won grudging admiration; some of the emotion aroused by human-rights atrocities has remained.

In 1948, Bavaria made headlines by rejecting the terms of the new German Constitution. Although the constitution was ratified, Bavaria was able to retain its title of 'Free State', as well as certain other unique privileges. Since then, the state has continued to dance to the beat of a different drummer – namely, for many years, Franz-Josef Strauss, who led Bavaria's own right-wing political party, the CSU, until his death in 1988. Conservative or no, Bavaria has prospered. After the war, many companies relocated from East Germany or no-longer-central Berlin to Bavaria, helping to build the state into a centre for science, commerce, industry, and the media.

The BMW office building in Munich

For all of its 'otherness', it's hard to characterise 'Bavaria' as a whole. Today's state represents one-fifth of the total land mass of Germany. Within this huge area are a wealth of contrasts, of landscapes, moods, flavours. 'Bavaria' is everything from the rural isolation of farming communities in the Bavarian Forest to the medieval perfection of a city like Bamberg; from the tradition of its folk customs to the high-tech of companies like BMW.

Perhaps no outsider like myself will ever quite be able to take for granted things which, to Bavarians, seem perfectly normal: the elaborate wall paintings on the houses of Alpine villages, or city streets which have remained basically unchanged since 1500. Yet Bavaria, for all of these 'fairy-tale' elements, is very real indeed. Most of its old cities and historic buildings are the backdrop to an active, modern daily life; few have become museum pieces for tourists. The past is a part of life here, to be lived with and built on. Even after the destruction caused by World War II Bavaria picked itself up out of the rubble and rebuilt its cities, complete with monuments old and new dedicated to distant glories and the promise not to repeat more recent nightmares. And life goes on.

Historical Highlights

500,000–700,000BC First people in Bavaria.

700–500BC Advent of Celts.

15BC Romans conquer the region in a single summer.

AD402 Start of Roman pull-out.

493 Theodoric establishes the Ostrogoth Empire.

788 Tassilo III, the last of the Agilolfing Dukes, is deposed by Charlemagne, and Bavaria is incorporated into the Carolingian Empire.

817 The Empire is partitioned, and Bavaria is placed under the control of 13-year-old King Ludwig 'the German'.

1156 The duchy of Bavaria is separated from the rest of the *Ostmark* (Eastern Marches of the Empire).

1180 Frederick I Barbarossa awards Bavaria to Otto I of the Wittelsbach family.

1214 The Upper Palatinate (*Oberpfalz*) is awarded to Bavaria.

1506 Splintered through being divided among ducal descendants, Bavaria is reunited when the law of primogeniture passed by Duke Albrecht IV empowers only first-born sons to rule.

1623 Bavaria becomes an Electorate under Maximilian I.

1648 End of the Thirty Years' War.

1803 'Secularisation': 131 monasteries are dissolved and many are destroyed.

1805 Bavarian Foreign Minister Montgelas signs treaty with Napoleon.

1806 Bavaria becomes a Kingdom; Elector Max IV Joseph becomes King Max I.

1808 Montgelas writes first Bavarian constitution.

1818 Constitution revised; two-chamber parliament implemented.

1848 Abdication of King Ludwig I.

1871 German Empire proclaimed: Bavaria is a member state, but Prussia leads.

1886 'Mad' King Ludwig II drowns mysteriously in Lake Starnberg.

1914 Declaration of war; start of World War I.

1918 King Ludwig III abdicates, ending 738 years of Wittelsbach rule.

1919 Murder of Socialist leader Kurt Eisner; short-lived soviet Republic of Bavaria. Parliamentary democracy begins.

1920 The city of Coburg votes itself into Bavaria.

1923 With the 'Beer Hall Putsch', the Nazis under Adolf Hitler try unsuccessfully to overthrow of the Bavarian government.

1933 Bavaria loses state autonomy.

1938 Synagogues and Jewish businesses attacked and ravaged. Austria and Czech Sudetenland annexed to Germany.

1939 German invasion of Poland; outbreak of World War II.

1940–45 Nazi massacre of German Jews. Munich, Nuremberg, Würzburg, Augsburg, and other cities devastated in Allied bombing raids.

1943 The *Weisse Rose*, the anti-Nazi resistance movement at Munich University fails, and the leaders Hans and Sophie Scholl are executed.

1945 Germany capitulates.

1948 German Constitution drawn up at Herrenchiemsee.

1949 Bavaria rejects the German Federal Republic's Constitution; as two-thirds of member states ratify it, it passes anyway.

1972 Munich hosts the Olympic Games.

1988 Death of Franz-Josef Strauss.

1989 The Berlin Wall falls, paving the way for German reunification.

1992 In December in Munich the first *Lichterkette* (candle vigils) protesting against violence to foreigners and minorities. 400,000 people take part.

Day itiner

Bavaria is quite simply a huge place. Over the years, the historic centre of the state – the provinces of Upper and Lower Bavaria and Upper Palatinate – has been enlarged by the addition of Franconia and part of Swabia. Today's Bavaria covers an area of 70,554 sq km (27,238 sq miles) – one-fifth of Germany's total land mass.

To enable the visitor to get the most out of a short trip, I have selected four key areas within the seven Bavarian provinces. In each area, I've designed day-long itineraries which include the best views of Bavaria's landscapes as well as visits to the region's beautiful old cities. For most rural routes you will need a car; city itineraries can all be accessed by train.

With Munich, the Bavarian capital, as the point of departure, the first of the four key areas covered by the itineraries is the province most visitors equate with 'Bavaria': **Upper Bavaria** (*Oberbayern*), including the Alps and King Ludwig's castles. To the west is the **Romantic Road** (*Romantische Strasse*), so called because of the in-credibly romantic qualities of the well-preserved medieval towns through which it passes on its way to Würzburg in **Franconia**. The sights of this province also include the Gothic splendours of Bam-berg as well as the striking rock formations of its own 'Little Switzerland' (*Fränkische Schweiz*). The last itineraries focus on rus-tic **Lower Bavaria** (*Niederbayern*), with the rolling woods and green vistas of the Bavarian Forest (*Bayerischer Wald*).

To follow all of these itineraries takes about two weeks and involves a lot of driv-ing. Ideally, however, the book also enables you to select your options. No matter where you choose, Bavaria is a region for all tastes and interests.

1. The Bavarian Capital

A day of sightseeing in the Bavarian capital: from the Electoral Residence to Marienplatz at the city centre via the city's art museums to the 'bohemian' neighbourhood of Schwabing and the English Garden.

'World City with Heart' (*Weltstadt mit Herz*) is one slogan often used to describe Munich; 'village of millions' (*Millionendorf*) is another. The real city lies somewhere between these two extremes of a cosmopolitan urban centre and a welcoming, relaxed small town. Dating back to the 1100s, when a monastery was established on the salt route from Italy and Austria, the city has retained its old-fashioned charm while keeping pace with international trends in business, art and fashion.

Start your tour of Munich at the open square of **Odeonsplatz**, where the main boulevard of Ludwigstrasse runs into the downtown pedestrian zone. Before you stand the arches of the neoclassical **Feldherrnhalle**, modelled on a loggia in Florence, where Hitler marched with his followers in an unsuccessful bid for power in 1923. To your left is the entrance to the

The Theatinerkirche

21

Outside the Cuvilliés Theatre

formal 17th-century **Hofgarten** (Court Garden); on your right, the yellow facade of the first piece of Bavarian baroque: St Cajetan, better known as **Theatinerkirche**. The latter wasn't the work of Bavarians, however; the Elector's Italian wife Henriette Adelaide, who commissioned the church from Italian builders in 1633, averred that the Bavarians were 'too idiotic' to undertake such a project.

Walk down Residenzstrasse to your left, past the **Residenz** (Electoral Residence). The reigning Wittelsbach family began construction on this site in 1385; successive generations made alterations to suit their needs and reflect their glory. As a result, the building – which houses several museums – is so large that it would take a day to see it in its entirety. I suggest you limit your tour to the marvellous **Cuvilliés Theatre**, a red-and-gold baroque extravaganza, and the **Antiquarium**, an impressive, 69-metre-long (226-ft) Renaissance room which spendthrift Duke Albrecht V built in 1571 to house the Electoral Library. The same Duke founded the **Schatzkammer** (Treasury), today containing a vast and valuable collection. The Residence's south facade, modelled on Florence's Pitti Palace, was built by architect Leo von Klenze for Ludwig I in 1835; Klenze was also responsible for rebuilding the nearby **National Theatre**, Munich's opera house, when the five-year-old building burnt to the ground in 1823.

Continue along Residenzstrasse as it merges with part of the **Fußgängerzone** (pedestrian precinct) leading to central **Marienplatz**. Here, amid fountains and flowers, shoppers push past tourists waiting for the famous **Glockenspiel**, a mechanical clock whose

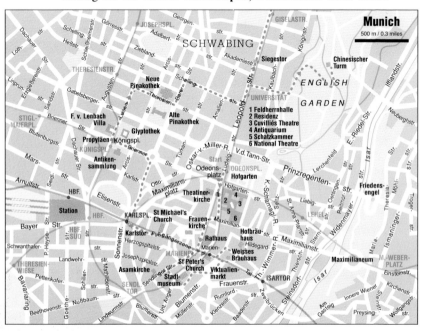

carved figures dance and even joust (daily at 11am, in summer also at noon and 5pm) in their niches on the ornate neo-Gothic facade of the **Neues Rathaus** (New Town Hall), which wasn't actually completed until 1908. The gilded **Madonna** in the square was erected in 1638 by Duke Maximilian I in thanks that Munich was spared in the Thirty Years' War.

Behind one corner of the square, **St Peter's Church**, the oldest in Munich, contains art treasures and a tower with a magnificent view of the city and surroundings. You can also get a bird's-eye view from the sixth-floor **Café Glockenspiel** (entrance to its lift is around the corner on Rosenstrasse), where I suggest you have coffee and cake at eye level with the mechanical clock.

After coffee, go down Rosenstrasse which leads south to the consumer paradise of Sendlingerstrasse; a few minutes' stroll will bring you to the church of St Johannes of Nepomuk, better known as the **Asamkirche**. A tiny space crammed with sculptures and gold leaf, this 1735 church is one of the more lavish, not to say startling, works of baroque artists Egid Quirin and Cosmas Damian Asam. Whether you find it marvellous or in poor taste, it's definitely worth a look.

Go back up Sendlingerstrasse and turn right to get to Oberanger. On the other side of the street is the marvellous, eclectic **Stadtmuseum** (Munich City Museum, Tuesday–Sunday 10am–5pm), whose exhibitions range from modern painting to city history (including the wooden Morris dancers carved in the 15th century to ornament the Old Town Hall). Left on Oberanger and right on Rosental, you come to **Viktualienmarkt**, a farmer's market selling everything from Italian salami to French cheeses, while locals clad in folk costume quaff beer and eat *Wurst* at outdoor tables.

Walking up the street by the market brings you to bustling **Tal** where, if the sight of all that food has made you hungry, you can stop in for lunch at the **Weisses Brauhaus** (Im Tal 10, Tel: 089-29 98 75), serving cuisine that's as authentically Bavarian as the surroundings. True Münchners come here at 11am to eat *Weisswurst*, a speciality of the city. If you go up Sparkassenstrasse, a right turn followed by a left will bring you to the famous **Hofbräuhaus**, offering similar food and ambience on a larger scale, but catering more to a tourist crowd.

Artiste in the pedestrian precinct

Strolling back through Marienplatz after lunch, note the distinctive twin towers of the **Frauenkirche** (Church of Our Lady) towering behind the buildings lining the pedestrian precinct of Kaufingerstrasse. When the towers were still roofless 30 years after the church's consecration in 1495, these unique round domes were erected as a temporary solution, and became so popular that they were retained. Also of interest is the Renaissance interior of **St Michael's**, a Jesuit building from the late 16th century, on your right as you walk along the precinct. In summer, the street is crowded not only with shoppers, but also with performers, including a variety of mime artists and itinerant musicians. Ahead of you, the arch of **Karlstor**, a reconstruction of a gate in the former city walls, frames the white spume of the fountain, surrounded by people cooling their heels.

Turn to the right and walk along busy Sonnenstrasse until you can cross over to the tram stop to board tram number 18 (direction Petuelring). Travelling slowly through the heart of the city, trams are a great way to see Munich. When you see the dark stone obelisk

Exhibits in the Glyptothek

at the centre of Karolinenplatz, get off the tram and go to Briennerstrasse; you'll recognise it by the monumental archway looming up ahead of you at the end of **Königsplatz**.

Originally the work of architect von Klenze (who was kept busy by the commissions of King Ludwig I), this square saw a less glorious period when it was paved and used as a parade ground by the Nazis in the 1930s. Today, it's been restored to its original grassy self, remaining a monument to Classicism in all its forms. In addition to the arch, called the **Propyläen**, there's the **Antikensammlung**, a collection of vases and other antiquities, and the **Glyptothek** (Tuesday, Wednesday, Friday–Sunday 10am–4.30pm; Thursday noon–8.30pm), one of my favourites, a beautiful, not-too-large museum displaying sculptures of ancient Greece and Rome.

Beyond the Propyläen, turn right up Luisenstrasse; almost immediately, you'll come upon the entrance to painter **Franz von Lenbach's villa**. This elegant residence is today a museum (Tuesday–Sunday 10am–6pm, Thursday until 8pm) of 19th-century German painting and modern exhibits as well as a remarkable collection of works of the Expressionist *Blaue Reiter* ('Blue Rider') school, a group of Munich-based artists including Wassily Kandinsky, Franz Marc and Paul Klee.

Munich's two main art museums can be found up Luisenstrasse and right on Theresienstrasse. The first of these, the **Alte Pinakothek**

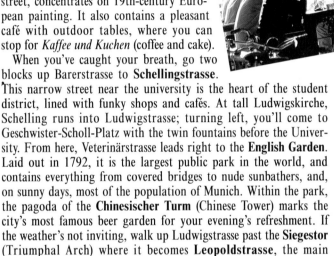

In the beer garden

(Tuesday–Sunday 9.15am–4.30pm, Tuesday and Thursday also 7–9pm), is yet another Leo von Klenze edifice housing the magnificent painting collection of the Wittelsbach family, Old Master works with an emphasis on Dutch and Flemish schools (its collection of Rubens paintings is perhaps the finest in the world). The **Neue Pinakothek** (Tuesday–Sunday 9.15am–4.30pm, Tuesday and Thursday also 7–9pm), across the street, concentrates on 19th-century European painting. It also contains a pleasant café with outdoor tables, where you can stop for *Kaffee und Kuchen* (coffee and cake).

When you've caught your breath, go two blocks up Barerstrasse to **Schellingstrasse**. This narrow street near the university is the heart of the student district, lined with funky shops and cafés. At tall Ludwigskirche, Schelling runs into Ludwigstrasse; turning left, you'll come to Geschwister-Scholl-Platz with the twin fountains before the University. From here, Veterinärstrasse leads right to the **English Garden**. Laid out in 1792, it is the largest public park in the world, and contains everything from covered bridges to nude sunbathers, and, on sunny days, most of the population of Munich. Within the park, the pagoda of the **Chinesischer Turm** (Chinese Tower) marks the city's most famous beer garden for your evening's refreshment. If the weather's not inviting, walk up Ludwigstrasse past the **Siegestor** (Triumphal Arch) where it becomes **Leopoldstrasse**, the main artery through bohemian **Schwabing**, with plenty of sidewalk cafés, restaurants, bars and discos where you can while away the night.

If you decide you want to stay another day in Munich, there are plenty more sights to see, including the magnificent Nymphenburg Palace to the west of the city and the futuristic Olympic Park to the north, created for the 1972 Olympic Games. Located on an island in the Isar near the city centre is the **Deutsche Museum**, a marvellous museum of science and technology.

The English Garden

Upper Bavaria

Nowhere is Bavaria more picturesque than in the region of Upper Bavaria, its villages bright with paintings and flowers, its inhabitants dressed in the quaint local costumes of their

Mountains over Mittenwald

forbears, its lakes reflecting the splendour of the surrounding mountains. Every one of these villages, furthermore, is the starting point of well-marked walking trails, from easy to arduous, which afford yet another perspective on the region, as well as a breath of the invigorating mountain air. The itineraries that follow are intended to reveal the best of Upper Bavaria, including such key destinations as Neuschwanstein Castle, Oberammergau, Garmisch, Mittenwald, Bavaria's best known lake the Chiemsee, and the resort town of Berchtesgaden. Travellers should ideally have their own transport, but access to the key sights of each itinerary is also possible by public transport.

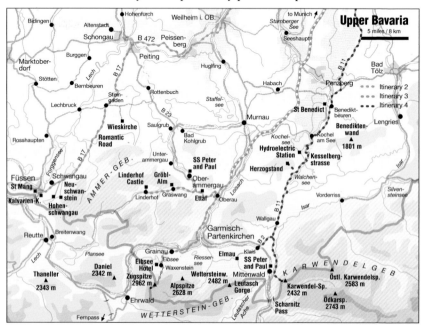

2. Füssen and the Royal Castles

Mad King Ludwig's medieval fantasy, the turreted castle of Neuschwanstein, and nearby Hohenschwangau, where he grew up; on to the town of Füssen, with its own old castle, medieval monastery, and charming Altstadt beside the blue river Lech.

From Munich, Füssen and Ludwig's castles are best reached by taking the *Autobahn* to Starnberg, the B2 to Weilheim, and from there the B472 to the B17, the southern section of the route called the *Romantische Strasse* (Romantic Road, *see p 42*). Having arrived in the hill resort of **Steingaden**, turn left out of the village and after about 3km (2 miles) go right down a narrow road (signed 'Wies') to the **Wieskirche**, considered to be one of the finest examples of Bavarian baroque. Built to house a miraculous image of Mary whose eyes shed real tears, the little church standing innocuously in its meadow was the work of the great baroque artist Johann Baptist Zimmermann, and is today a site of pilgrimage for art lovers as well as worshippers.

Cherub in the Wieskirche

Return to Steingaden and continue along the B17. As the Alps loom ever nearer on the horizon (weather permitting), watch for roads to the left marked *Königsschlößer* (King's Castles). The castles in question will be visible as soon as you turn off, rising from their wooded slopes. Lower, and to the right, is yellow Hohenschwangau; on the left is the higher, grey, soaring shape familiar from picture postcards and Walt Disney logos: **Neuschwanstein**. No matter how often you've seen it, 'mad' King Ludwig II's fairy-tale castle never loses its unreal, other-worldly air. Perhaps this is because it never was quite 'real': an anachronism when it was built from 1869–86 (and never finished), the castle was only inhabited for a matter of days, and therefore its only tangible function for its entire existence has been that of a glorified stage set.

After the dramatic promise of its exterior, a tour of Neuschwanstein's interior is likely to be disappointing. Although horse-drawn carriages are available to spare you the steep, 25-minute ascent on foot from the car park in Hohenschwangau, there's no way to avoid the lines of tourists, which in the summer months often reach through the gate.

Neuschwanstein in the mist

Hohenschwangau Castle

Unless you're a real castle fan, avoid the crowded heights altogether, and head instead to a castle which really was inhabited, and still is: **Hohenschwangau**, on the other side of the valley. The ascent doesn't take more than five minutes; guided tours are given 8.30am–5.30pm (November–March 10am–4pm). Ludwig spent much of his youth in this castle, built as a summer palace by his father between 1835 and 1855. Inside, it preserves relics of the historical past ranging from cannonballs to one of composer Richard Wagner's pianos. One wing of the building still serves as a summer home to descendants of the Wittelsbach family.

The Alpenstrasse leads to **Füssen**, 4km (2½ miles) away. Dating back to Roman times, later reclaimed by the Irish monks who arrived in Bavaria spreading Catholicism in the 8th and 9th century, this historic old town is in my opinion every bit as interesting to visit as the more famous castles nearby. In fact, it has its own medieval castle perched above the town, as well as the monastery founded by the Irish monk Magnus, St Mang in local parlance, on the banks of the river Lech. The ascent to the **castle**, former Residence of the Prince-Bishops of Augsburg, is worthwhile for a look at its Gothic courtyard, the only one in Germany, with its unique *trompe l'oeil* painting. At the foot of its hill stands the **monastery church**, a lovely piece of baroque free of some of the excesses of other contemporary buildings.

Winter near Füssen

Part of the monastery now serves as the **Rathaus** (Town Hall); off its main courtyard, you'll also find the interesting **City Museum** (*Museum der Stadt Füssen*; open April–October 11am–4pm, November–March 2pm–4pm, closed Monday). In addition to relics of the monks from Romanesque to baroque times and the **St Anna** chapel with its striking Dance of Death (*Totentanz*) frescoes, the museum highlights the local craft of lute-making. In the Renaissance, Füssen was Germany's leading centre for this trade; as its strict, 12-member guild had no room for newcomers, apprentices who completed their training were forced to go elsewhere; many went south to Italy, where their skills flourished. From the lute was born such stringed instruments as the violin; Italian violin makers, some say, have Füssen to thank for the emergence of their craft.

As you walk toward the river from the Rathaus, you can see three crosses at the top of the mountain above you: the summit of an elaborate **Stations of the Cross**. Cross the river Lech and turn right; 200m (650ft) along to the left, the little **Church of our Lady** was the site where plague victims, who had to be buried out of town, were interred. Here begins the way up the mountain, past 12 little houses decorated by painters of the Nazarene school, a group of artists formed around 1810 who worked in a style based on the paintings of the Middle Ages.

The summit presents a superb panoramic view of the town and, in the other direction, Ludwig's castles. For the return route, follow paths to **Lechfall** – and even if you're not up to the 1½-hour walk to the summit and back, make sure you don't miss the sight of this broad, white waterfall thundering from the azure-blue Lech river. You can also witness the spectacle by simply continuing along Tirolerstrasse past the plague church.

If you're not in a hurry to go back to Munich or have arranged to stay in Füssen (see *Accommodation* in *Practical Information*), return along the Lech to the cobbled streets of the Old Town for dinner in the restaurant **Zum Schwanen**, housed in a 15th-century building (Brotmarkt 4, Tel: 08362-6174), or the more modest but tasteful **Tiroler Weinstube**, upstairs at Franziskanergasse 1 (Tel: 08362-6259).

Relaxing at Albsee

From the murals and flowers on the house fronts of Oberammergau via Linderhof, King Ludwig's favourite castle, to Lake Eibsee at the foot of Germany's highest mountain, the Zugspitze, with its magnificent views.

'I thought I was in Disneyland,' said an American friend of his first sight of **Oberammergau**; and indeed, this little village seems almost too pretty to be real. Reached by taking the Garmisch *Autobahn* from Munich, then turning right after Oberau onto the B23 (1–1½ hours' drive altogether), Oberammergau is overshadowed by grey, rocky peaks, surrounded by green meadows, with its typical painted houses alternating with brown barns where cows quietly chew their

Facade with 'Lüftlmalerei'

cud. Inhaling deeply (preferably at a safe distance from the cows), you can understand why the cool, bracing air of the mountains is said to have healing properties, and why Oberammergau, like so many other villages in the Alps, is an official health resort (*Luftkurort*) where people come not, as in other fashionable resorts, to give themselves airs, but to take them.

As you walk through the streets of the town, take special note of the house facades. The art of *Lüftlmalerei* (airy painting), the facade frescoes of historical or religious subjects seen in so many Bavarian towns, originated in Oberammergau. Although houses were painted before his day, Franz Zwinck (1748–92) boosted the custom from quaint tradition to a recognised form of folk art.

Walking up Dorfstrasse from the church, turn left onto Verlegergasse toward the **Pilatus House**, a major work of Zwinck's from 1784, restored in 1909. Today, the lavishly decorated house contains a shop, and, in summer, a workshop where various artisans – wood-cutters, jewellers, and the like – practice their trade for the benefit of visitors.

Leaving the Pilatus House, follow Steinbachergasse over Dorfstrasse to the **Passionsspielhaus** (Playhouse) where, every ten years, the town's famous Passion Play is performed. The 6-hour retelling of the life and passion of Christ, cast with local villagers, is staged as the result of a vow made in 1633: the plague had struck, and the townspeople pledged to perform the play if the Lord would spare their village from annihilation. The next performance will take place in the year 2000; until then, permanent exhibits about the play are on display at the playhouse (9.30am–12pm and 1.30pm–4.30pm, closed Monday).

If it wasn't already clear from numerous shops you passed on your way through town, sculptures for sale in the theatre lobby will make you aware of the fact that Oberammergau is also a centre for the regional craft of wood-carving. Before retracing your route on the B23, look in on the little rococo **church of SS Peter and Paul** on Pfarrplatz.

After about 3km (2 miles), take the right-hand turnoff to Graswang and Linderhof, and drive 9km (5 miles) through the tranquil valley to **Linderhof Castle** (open year-round, during summer 9am–5.30pm; October–March 10am–4pm; closed 12.15–12.45pm. Grotto closed in winter). The best of King Ludwig's castles – and the only one he actually completed – Linderhof, built between 1870 and 1877, was inspired by French models, a sharp contrast to the German heritage of Neuschwanstein. Surrounded by fountains and a formal French garden, it includes such features as an underground grotto, complete with fake 'stalactites' and a lake, where the eccentric King was fond of watching private performances of Wagner operas.

From Linderhof, go back towards the B23; before Graswang, on the left, is the steep uphill driveway of the restaurant **Gröbl-Alm** (Tel: 08822-6434), where you can eat a hearty Bavarian lunch looking down over the green valley and the Alps.

As you drive back towards the B23, you're following the route taken by Ludwig the Bavarian in 1330; returning from the trip to Rome on which he was crowned Holy Roman Emperor with something less than unanimous approval, Ludwig was riding through this valley when his horse fell to its knees; taking this a sign from Heaven, the Emperor vowed to found a Benedictine monastery on the site. The result, **Kloster Ettal**, lies 1km east of the junction on the B23. If you want to look in at the round domed church,

'baroque-ised' in the mid-18th century, you can pick up a few bottles of Ettal beer as a souvenir; the monastery is one of the few in Bavaria which has managed to preserve its traditional brewery and distillery.

As you drive south towards **Garmisch** on

In Linderhof Castle gardens

Garmisch-Partenkirchen 18km
Oberau 8 km

Oberammergau 3km

Ettal 3km

the B23, you may see a paraglider or two spiralling earthward from the mountain heights. One of the central resorts in the Alps, host to the 1936 Winter Olympics – the ski jump and stadium are still in evidence – Garmisch is a prime destination for sportsmen of all descriptions: paragliders, walkers, skaters and skiers (who flock to the Zugspitz-platt, Germany's only skiable glacier). The presence of hordes of American servicemen partly explains the McDonald's, Pizza Hut, and comfortable English-language cinema on the main street, looking rather incongruous among houses sporting *Lüftlmalerei* epigrams and murals.

Once you've seen the town, signs to Grainau/Eibsee will direct you to the right, through part of central Garmisch and on out toward jagged grey Alps which seem to rise directly from the valley floor. Left through **Grainau**, the road leads 10km (6 miles) through pastures and meadows to little **Eibsee**, a lake tucked in amongst the pines at the foot of Germany's tallest mountain, the **Zugspitze**. By the lake is the station for the cable car (*Eibsee-Seilbahn*); if you've a head for heights, buy a return ticket and board one of the bright red cars, looking like childrens' toys, which leave every half-hour for the 10-minute ascent high over the craggy slopes to the summit. At 2,964m (9,724ft), the Zugspitze is neatly divided by the Austrian border, but Germany still has claim to at least half of it. From the station at the top, it's a short walk to the cross at the peak (*Spitze*) and the highest view in all of Germany.

The summit of the Zugspitze

At the foot of the mountain, on the lake, the **Eibsee Hotel** (Tel: 08821-8081), which was once patronised by the likes of Thomas Mann and other artistic and literary figures seeking a weekend's respite from Munich, has maintained its charm, even if its prices have risen over the years. The restaurant, its lakeside balcony commanding a marvellous view of the Zugspitze, offers fine dining for a pretty penny; if you're not up to a splurge, go in at around 4pm, when you can order coffee, select a piece of cake from the ample cake buffet, and eat in the fresh air, watching the late afternoon light wink off the cable cars and the grey slopes of the mountain.

32

4. Kesselbergstrasse and Mittenwald

Along scenic Kesselberg Road, trade route of the Renaissance, to a one-time centre of transalpine commerce, the beautiful village of Mittenwald.

In 1492, the monks of the **Benediktbeuren** monastery were assigned responsibility for maintaining a considerable stretch of a road that was, in every sense of the word, trail-blazing. The Tyrol, today in Austria and northern Italy, was an important centre of trade in the Middle Ages and Renaissance, a halfway point between the merchants of mighty Venice and their eager customers to the north. Access to the Tyrol from Munich, however, was difficult; the narrow 'King's Path' between the lakes Walchensee and Kochelsee, dating from 1120, was inadequate, and the only other choices were the narrow Isar Valley or the road through the Murnau Swamp, which was all too prone to flooding.

The problem of transportation became acute in 1487, when the hot-tempered Duke of Tyrol arrested 130 Venetian merchants and declared war on the Republic of Venice. The Venetians promptly took their business elsewhere: to the Bavarian town of Mittenwald, which became a flourishing trade centre. For residents of Munich, access to the region was now of even greater importance.

So, at least, thought Heinrich Barth, who had been prospecting for ore, unsuccessfully, in the area of Kochelsee. Barth oversaw the construction of a road, called **Kesselbergstrasse**, hailed even today as an engineering marvel. Now paved, it still makes its winding way across the heights; a roadside plaque pays tribute to Barth's skill and the financial backing of Bavarian Duke Albrecht IV (who, coincidentally, was the one who urged the Tyrolean duke to declare war on Venice in the first place).

Driving south from Munich on the B11, to the south of Benediktbeuren you'll find the beginning of what's known as Kesselbergstrasse by the flat expanse of **Kochelsee**, where there's a museum devoted to painter **Franz Marc** (open 1 April–31 October and over Christmas) in the town of **Kochel am See**. After Kochel, a series of zig-zags leads you up one mountainside – a lay-by to the right affords a panoramic view of the flat plain stretching away behind you – and down another to a lake of a different colour, **Walchensee**, surrounded by Alps and crowded, in fine weather, with windsurfers. Walchensee is 158m (518ft) higher than Kochelsee, a fact which inspired engineer Oskar von Miller, the

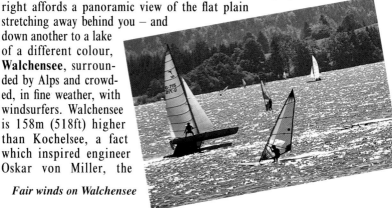

Fair winds on Walchensee

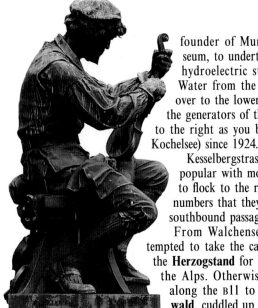
Matthias Klotz monument

founder of Munich's Deutsche Museum, to undertake the building of a hydroelectric station by Kochelsee. Water from the higher lake is piped over to the lower lake, and has driven the generators of the plant (immediately to the right as you begin the ascent from Kochelsee) since 1924.

Kesselbergstrasse's hairpin bends are popular with motorcyclists, who used to flock to the road in such daredevil numbers that they've been barred from southbound passage on weekends.

From Walchensee, you may well be tempted to take the cable car to the top of the **Herzogstand** for a magnificent view of the Alps. Otherwise, continue straight along the B11 to the town of **Mittenwald**, cuddled up against the grey flank of the Karwendel mountain range. As a drive through the surrounding countryside demonstrates (left on the B2 towards Klais, and from there follow signs to **Elmau** to come to a valley whose scenery merits a bit of a detour), Mittenwald has one of the most stunning locations of any village in the Alps. The town itself is fully lovely enough to do justice to its surroundings. Rows of brightly painted houses attest to the fact that Mittenwald has historically been yet another centre for *Lüftlmalers*; a particularly talented local son, Franz Karner, is responsible for facades such as that of the **Neunerhaus** on **Obermarkt**. At one end of this street, where Bavarian restaurants and artisans' shops predominate, a grassy plot of wildflowers supports gnarled apple trees, laden with blossom or green fruit in the spring and summer; at the other end, where Obermarkt meets Hochstrasse, is the **Church of SS Peter and Paul**, a lovely little 18th-century Rococo building with a beautifully frescoed tower.

Before the church there's a monument to the violin maker **Matthias Klotz**. A devoted musician, Klotz went south to Italy to study violin-making in Cremona with the master Amati (Stradivarius's teacher), then wandered about Europe for a few decades before finally returning home to Mittenwald, bringing the tools of his trade with him. His efforts made the town even more renowned than Füssen as the capital of German stringed instrument making, a craft alive and well today (the town's school of violin-making trains apprentices from all over the world). If you would like more detailed idea of the history and practice of this art, then I would strongly recommend a visit to the **Geigenbaumuseum** (Museum of Violin-Making) down narrow and picturesque Ballenhausgasse behind the church (Monday–Friday 10am–11.45am, 2pm–4.45pm; Saturday–Sunday and holidays 10am–11.45am).

Two forms of sustenance

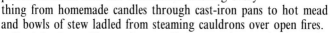

Seemingly inspired by the curves of the violin, the tower of the Gothic church of **St Nicholas**, on Untermarkt, is another of Mittenwald's landmarks. In July, you can get a real taste of life in the Renaissance during the town's two-week **Renaissance Festival**, at which vendors, artisans and artists in period costume line the Obermarkt offering everything from homemade candles through cast-iron pans to hot mead and bowls of stew ladled from steaming cauldrons over open fires.

Straight down Obermarkt, a well-signposted route leads to the **Leutasch Gorge**, where a wooden walkway leads to a remarkable waterfall – technically in Austria, but one doesn't split hairs in this border town. Even more breathtaking is another remarkable view to which Austria can also lay claim – that from the top of the **Karwendel Spitze**, accessible by a cable car leaving from the station (about ten minutes' walk from Obermarkt, behind the railway station) every half hour (8.30am–4pm). The ride's not long, and the view's spectacular (provided the mountain's not in cloud); you can snack at the café atop the mountain. Or save your appetite for dinner at the **Alpenrose** (Obermarkt 1, Tel: 08823-5055), one of Mittenwald's oldest, and most atmospheric, restaurants.

Mittenwald's magnificent setting

5. Chiemsee

On a ferry round the islands of the largest lake in Bavaria where you can see an 8th-century convent, a gorgeous little fishing village, and yet another of King Ludwig's fantastic castles.

The A8, otherwise known as the Salzburg Autobahn, has got to be one of the most beautiful motorways in the world. Not overly wide,

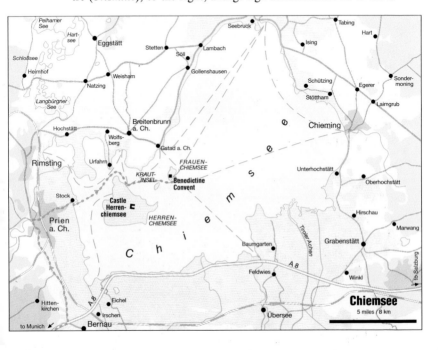

it winds through rolling countryside, past onion-domed churches and red-roofed villages toward a backdrop of the Alps at their most spectacular.

About an hour and a half from Munich, the route runs along the shores of a flat silver plain of water, wrinkled by sailboats and windsurfers, with now and then a hot-air balloon hovering overhead. This is the lake of **Chiemsee**, at 80 sq km (31 sq miles) Bavaria's largest, drawing holiday-makers from all over Germany for sailing, swimming, and other summer pursuits.

To get to the lake, turn off at the Bernau exit (also marked Prien), and follow signs right to **Prien**. Hidden behind the trees, Chiemsee already sheds a silver, liquid light; car parks, campgrounds and hotels

A church along the A8

called 'Am See' are indication of its proximity. After about 5km (3 miles), the railway lines and the road lead off left to the town centre (*Ortsmitte*); to the right, a large sign announces ferries to the is-

lands and parking for the restaurants and hotels that constitute the settlement of **Stock**. Past a station for the toy-like green steam train that's run since 1887 between the lake and the town of Prien 2km (1 mile) away are the landings for the passenger boats – some of them complete with paddle wheels – out to the islands of Herrenchiemsee and Frauenchiemsee.

Whatever you may think of 'mad' King Ludwig II, no one can say he didn't have an eye for a beautiful setting. In fact, though, he found **Herrenchiemsee**, the island he bought in 1873, unattractive, and hoped to improve its appearance by building a perfect replica of Louis XIV's Versailles. Ludwig, alas, didn't have the funds available to the Sun King (although Louis had modestly limited himself to *one* palace), and only the central wing of the building could be completed before his death in 1886.

Disembarking from the ferry, you will pass a beer garden overlooking the water and the 'old castle', the buildings which housed the Augustinian monastery which originally occupied the island. After a 15-minute walk through woodland and pasture you will see the **castle's** yellow facade through the trees. Complete with marble reception foyer and a magnificent *Spiegelsaal* (Hall of Mirrors), the castle can be visited on half-hour tours through-out the day (until 5pm). If you've already seen enough of Ludwig's castles, you may want to content yourself with strolling through the gardens, exploring the island, or visiting the 'old palace', which hosts temporary exhibits in its elegant baroque library. It was here that political leaders met to thrash out the details of the German constitution in 1948.

The '*Spiegelsaal*'

From Herrenchiemsee, the ferry route leads past uninhabited Krautinsel, which used to function as a common garden area for the monks and nuns, to **Frauenchiemsee**, where Duke Tassilo III founded a **convent** for Benedictine nuns in 782. The first thing you see as you get off the boat is a sea of flowers; the flowers and

37

In the graveyard at Frauenchiemsee

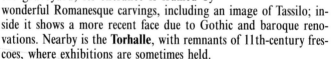

herbs used to distill the liqueurs you can buy in the convent shop are all still grown in the convent garden. Today the convent is in use as a boarding school for women studying home economics and child-rearing, and is not open to visitors; but its little church is. Facing the graveyard, its entrance is framed by wonderful Romanesque carvings, including an image of Tassilo; inside it shows a more recent face due to Gothic and baroque renovations. Nearby is the **Torhalle**, with remnants of 11th-century frescoes, where exhibitions are sometimes held.

The island isn't just a convent; it's also home to a small fishing community, and, in recent years, to artists eager for a piece of Fraueninsel's tranquil beauty. At the other end of the island (which is only 600m/1,950ft long and 300m/980ft wide), wander the narrow lanes between the lush banks of flowers which overflow the gardens of every house along the way. Some of these flower-bedecked homes house purveyors of smoked fish (*Räucherfisch*), guest rooms (*Gästezimmer*), or even the island's traditional ceramicist (*Töpferei*), his store windows filled with his work. Take some time to walk around the island, stopping for a meal in the **Gasthof Inselwirt** (Tel: 08054-630) on the water or taking a dip from one of the small beaches before getting on the boat again to continue, either on the 'Grosse Tour' around the whole lake, or back to Stock.

If you're driving late on the A8 in either direction, watch for the motorway rest stop at the Holzkirchen exit. Unlike the stereotypical highway eatery, which offers much the same sort of uninspired cafeteria-style food and ambience whether in Germany, England or the States, the **Bayrisches Rasthaus Holzkirchen** (Tel: 08024-1607) is a comfortable restaurant serving a wide range of excellent Bavarian food in an appropriately Bavarian atmosphere – a welcome sight to weary drivers returning late to Munich.

Sunset over the lake

6. Berchtesgaden

A tour of the salt mines; Berchtesgaden's Romanesque monastery; and a cruise on tranquil Königssee, the Alps' most beautiful lake.

To non-Germans, unfortunately, the name **Berchtesgaden** is linked with Hitler, who used his nearby home as a weekend retreat during the Third Reich. Actually, the town has closer associations with a certain Mr Perther. About a thousand years ago, Perther built a house (called, in Old German, *Gaden*) here; over the years, Perther's Gaden has been metamorphosed to Berchtesgaden.

The Watzmann towers over Berchtesgaden

Certainly, most of what's interesting about Berchtesgaden pre-dates World War II. Amidst some of the most spectacular scenery in the undeniably scenic Alpine region, the town's sloping streets sport not only the colourful facades common to many Alpine villages, but a number of stunning churches, an 11th-century monastery, and a baroque castle – all above average, even in a region as richly blessed with historical and architectural testimony as Bavaria.

To get to Berchtesgaden, leave the A8 at the Bad Reichenhall exit, and follow the B20. Once in town, you can park, if all else fails, in the underground car park at the city centre. You'll come out just by the **Kurpark**, a lush formal garden which reminds one that this is yet another of the Alps' many *Luftkurort* health resorts; a stroll in the garden is part of the cure. Indeed, the garden exudes a kind of heavy coolness; and its lushness contrasts oddly with the pastel facades which climb the steep cobbled streets.

Make sure you don't miss the opportunity of a visit to the **salt mines**, in operation since 1517. To get there from the garden, cross over Schießstättstrasse and follow

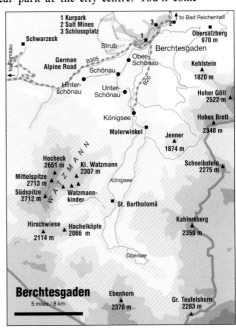

1 Kurpark
2 Salt Mines
3 Schlossplatz

to Bad Reichenhall

Obersalzberg
970 m

Berchtesgaden

Schwarzeck

Strub

to Ramsau

German
Alpine Road

B305

Ober-
Schönau

Schönau

Kehlstein
1820 m

Hinter-
schönau

Unter-
Schönau

B20

Hoher Göll
2522 m

Königsee

Hohes Brett
2340 m

Malerwinkel

Jenner
1874 m

Hocheck
2651 m

Kl. Watzmann
2307 m

Königsee

Schneibstein
2275 m

Mittelspitze
2713 m

Südspitze
2712 m

Watzmann-
kinder

St. Bartholomä

Hirschwiese
2114 m

Hachelköpfe
2066 m

Kahlersberg
2350 m

Obersee

Berchtesgaden

5 miles / 8 km

Ebenhorn
2370 m

Gr. Teufelshorn
2283 m

Downtown Berchtesgaden

Bräuhausstrasse out of town for about half a mile. In its heyday, this entire region had salt to thank for its economic prosperity; Bad Reichenhall, nearby, still gives its name to German table salt, while it's not hard to see where nearby Salzburg, in Austria, got its name ('salt fortress'). Today, the underground passage is safer than it used to be, and the mines are open to everyone (1½ hour tours 1 May–15 October daily 8.30am–5pm; 15 October–30 April Monday–Saturday 12.30pm–3.30pm, Tel: 08652-60020). Donning traditional mining garments, you'll descend into the depths; there, further descent is possible by means of slides (especially popular with children), and a boat will conduct you across a subterranean lake.

After you've seen the salt mines walk back to the town centre and the pedestrian zone on and around **Marktplatz**, a network of cobble-stoned streets with everything from handicrafts to grocer's shops. At one end of Marktplatz, a heavy, low arch admits both car and pedestrian traffic to the sudden quiet of **Schlossplatz** (Castle Square). Just before you is the elaborate portal of the **Abbey Church of SS Peter and John the Baptist**, built in 1122 of gold-grey stone; adjacent to this, around two sides of the irregularly-shaped 'square', is the pink facade of the castle itself, brocaded with elaborate white stucco work around the windows. Standing by the fountain and looking back in the direction you came, you can see, in striking contrast to this delicate baroque trim, the heavy arches of an arcade running along one side of the square, which was built as a granary in 1558.

The pastiche effect is continued in the interior of the Abbey Church, which has elements dating from every age between 1122 and 1866, when the towers were finally completed. Soaring columns support a vault suspended over an angular Gothic interior; along the right-hand wall, however, are baroque touches which clearly date from the 17th-century renovation of the castle for the *Fürstpropste* (Prince-priors).

Next door, the **castle** is a real treat. Monastery, royal residence, museum: each of these chapters in the building's history is reflected in some part of the existing architecture. In the cloister, fragile double columns support capitals with fanciful, whimsical carvings of men and animals, indication of the building's Romanesque origins and the Irish roots of Christianity in the region. From here, a flight of stairs leads up to the impressive arched hallway of the **Castle Museum**. Filled with art and armour, frescoes and furniture from medieval to baroque, the castle (guided tours 10am–1pm, 2pm–5pm;

Alpine attire

St Bartholomä stoops before the Watzmann

closed Saturday Easter–30 September, at weekends and holidays October–Easter) actually remained a Wittelsbach residence until the death of Crown Prince Rupprecht in 1955.

Head back to your car and follow the B20, which forks off to the left from the train station toward Schönau and Königssee. Walkers can cover the 3km (2 miles) to Königsee on foot, along a path which starts near the railway station and leads along the stream. Rising steeply to the left of the road is the peak of Hitler's 'Eagle's Nest' retreat, the **Kehlsteinhaus**.

Königssee, the King's Lake, is quite simply one of the most beautiful spots in the Alps. Flat, silent, mirror-still, the narrow lake is surrounded by mountains. You can see the lake from lookout points on shore, such as **Malerwinkel** (painter's corner), or one of the electric passenger boats which operate year-round (except when the lake is iced over). Although the **Watzmann** mountains (mother, father, and seven children) dominate the panorama from almost any vantage point, it is from the boat that you'll get one of the most stunning views. Halfway down the lake is the little chapel of **St Bartholomä**, its round domes outlined against one of the most beautiful backdrops you could hope to find. The summit of the Watzmann towers 2,100m (6,800ft) above, its giant east face the highest in the Eastern Alps. Rain or shine, there's something ethereal about this beautiful cruise. (Summer every 10–20 minutes 7.15am–6pm; pre- and post-season every 15–30 minutes after 8.15am; winter every 45 minutes after 9.15am).

Leaving Königssee, either retrace your steps or cut through the village of Schönau to get to the B305, the **German Alpine Road** (*Deutsche Alpenstrasse*). This scenic route winds through green valleys and wooded slopes along the Alps; you're heading towards the valley village of **Ramsau**, with its much-photographed jewel of a baroque church. Stay on the 305, however, and turn off to the right (following signs to Hochschwarzeck) up a zig-zagging road to the **Hotel-Gasthof Nutzkaser** (Tel: 08657-388), where you can enjoy a wonderful Bavarian meal 1,100m (3,600ft) above sea level, with a panoramic view of the mountains.

The Romantic Road

Reflections of Dinkelsbühl

When the sleepy, forgotten walled towns of medieval, half-timbered houses which dot Western Bavaria were rediscovered by 19th-century travellers, they rapidly became popular tourist spots where people could capture the flavour of days gone by. Today, the route leading from Ludwig's castles in the south to Würzburg in the north has been christened the 'Romantic Road'. From the road you can glimpse castle towers and church spires before driving into the towns themselves, still fundamentally unchanged, although the crush of tourism has made them appear a little less sleepy than they did a century ago. We have already covered the southern section of the route in itinerary 2; in the three day itineraries that follow, you can see some more of its most important highlights. We begin in Augsburg, once a powerful free city of the Holy Roman Empire, and continue northwards along the B25 through medieval Dinkelsbühl and Rothenburg and on to Würzburg, residence of a long line of prince-bishops and the home of Franconian wine.

7. Augsburg

A tour of the city from Renaissance town hall to Gothic cathedral; Europe's earliest council flats; the shops of medieval craftsmen; and the homes of Brecht, Holbein, and the family Mozart.

Founded in 15BC, Augsburg has gone through many ups and downs since Tacitus described it as the 'most splendid colony of the province of Rhaetium'. An independent city-state of the Holy Roman Empire since 1156, the city flourished in the Renaissance with such artisan trades as gold- and silversmithing; but its power gradually waned until Napoleon bequeathed it to Bavaria in 1806. In this century, World War II bombings virtually razed it to the ground. But rebuilders and restorers have been hard at work, and Augsburg today has both the narrow canals and ivy-draped city walls of the old city and, on the other hand, the businesses and commerce of a modern urban centre.

Augsburg's Town Hall

Start your tour of Augsburg at the square before the **Rathaus** (Town Hall); completed in 1620, it's one of Germany's major Renaissance constructions. Its architect, Elias Holl, also designed the neighbouring **Perlach Tower**, which you can climb (1 April–31 October) for a view of the city and its surroundings. In his 20 years as the city's master builder, Holl planned a number of major Augsburg buildings; but in 1631, he was ignominiously removed from office because he was Protestant – despite Ausgburg's historic position of religious tolerance.

At the centre of the square water splashes from one of three **fountains** commissioned for Augsburg's 1600th birthday – in 1589. The three statues depict Augustus, symbol of the city founders; Mercury (commerce and trade); and Hercules (Man's mastery of Nature): it's Augustus you see here.

Follow Karolinenstrasse north toward the city's magnificent **Cathedral** (*Dom*), begun in the 9th century, and redone in Gothic style in the 14th. The cast bronze plates on the door to the left of the main entrance, depicting Old Testament and various mythological scenes, are thought to date from around 1050. Inside, the stained-glass windows of the prophets in Jewish costume, supposedly installed when the church was renovated in 1140, are said to be the oldest in the world. You can also see some altar paintings by local son Hans Holbein the Elder.

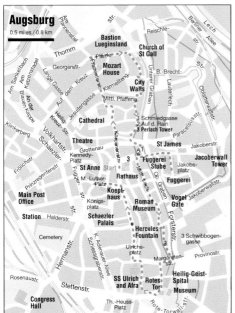

North along Frauentorstrasse is the **Mozart House**, today a museum, where Leopold Mozart, father of the composer Wolfgang Amadeus, was born and raised. Continue on to the street Pfärrle and turn right to come to the **Church of St Gall**, the oldest in Augsburg, built in 1051 and restored in the 15th century, sitting against the old **city walls**. It's more a matter of leg-

end than fact that Martin Luther escaped through the hole in the wall behind the church when he fled Augsburg in 1518; but the hole is there, plain to see.

Further south, past the 1504 house of painter Hans Burgkmair on your right, cross Leonhardsberg, and turn down Auf dem Rain, a narrow street of low terrace houses traversed by a miniature canal. In **house No 7**, playwright Bertolt Brecht was born in 1898. Today, there are art exhibits on the ground floor and a collection of Brecht memorabilia above (May–October 10am–5pm, November–April 10am–4pm, closed Monday).

Across the street (house number 6) and up the street (Schmiedgasse 15) are the Goldsmith's Shop and the Bookbinder's. These are two of the stops along Augsburg's **Artisan Route** (*Handwerkerweg*), a tour through workshops and stores where certain trades have been plied for centuries, including the violin-makers, the tannery, and the convent where nuns embroider clerical garments for festive High Masses. Not all of the stops along the route are open every day, but some observe normal business hours. For details, pick up the pamphlet *Ausburger Handwerkerweg* at the tourist office.

Barfüsserstrasse, to the left, leads to the entrance to the **Fuggerei**. Jakob Fugger (1459–1525), the scion of a prosperous family of businessmen, brought their already thriving empire to new heights. But Fugger was not just a money-bagging tycoon; as proof of this, he built the first council flats in Europe. Founded in 1516, this development for poor Catholics charged an annual rent of one florin for each three-room apartment, one condition being that residents say the Lord's Prayer every day for the souls of the Fuggers. Both the rent (DM1.72) and this condition have survived to the present day. For a local meal in a rustic atmosphere, try the **Fuggerei-Stube** (Jakoberstrasse 26, Tel: 0821-30870) for lunch.

Retrace your steps along Jakoberstrasse and Barfüsserstrasse before turning left down Mittlerer Lech for a stroll along the Lech canals

Afra's Cathedral

(which have run through the city since the days of the Romans), past old buildings like the 18th-century **Gignoux House**. To your left is the Gothic **Vogel Gate** in the city walls. Continue down Schwibbogengasse, past the water wheel; a short cut left off Margaretenstrasse leads to the **Heilig-Geist-Spital**, designed by the ubiquitous Holl, today home to the **Augsburg Puppet Theatre** and the **Swabian Crafts Museum** (highlight of the Artisan Route). A short walk brings you to the **Rotes Tor** (Red Gate), built in the 16th century as a defensive fortification to safeguard the vital trade route to Italy, and renovated according to Holl's designs in 1622. In the Middle Ages, a vital source of city water were the **Water Towers** on the left, which date back to the 1400s.

Up Ulrichsgasse, you'll come to the **Cathedral of St Ulrich and St Afra**. Afra ran a brothel in Augusta Vindelicorum in the 3rd century; one night, a Spanish bishop fleeing persecution in his own country took refuge in her establishment and converted her and her daughters to Christianity, and she became so zealous that she and her offspring were burnt at the stake in 304. Her remains are ensconced, together with those of Ulrich, in the crypt of her soaring cathedral. Ulrich, the first man to be canonised in the history of the Catholic church, gave his name to both this Catholic church and the adjacent, but much smaller, Protestant **Ulrich's Church**. The two churches are a nod to Augsburg's 1555 law of religious tolerance, which decreed that the ruler of the land had to choose one religion, and his subjects were obliged to follow him – a measure which predictably gave rise to no end of trouble.

Fountain detail

From Ulrichsplatz, broad Maximilianstrasse runs back toward the Town Hall. Across from the **Hercules Fountain** on the left is the **Schaezler Palais**, built by an 18th-century businessman. The yellow-fronted building houses a rococo festival hall, a marvellous staircase, and two museums, of which I find the **State Gallery**, featuring a portrait of Fugger by Albrecht Dürer, the more compelling.

At the Mercury Fountain, cut across the pedestrian zone to Martin-Luther-Platz and the **Church of St Anne**, a monastery which turned Protestant during the Reformation, and gave shelter to Martin Luther during his ill-starred visit to Augsburg in 1518; it now contains the well-known portrait of Luther by Lucas Cranach the Elder. Back on Karolinenstrasse, the **König von Flandern Brauerei** (downstairs at No 12, Tel: 0821-158050) serves snacks and its own home-brewed beer.

A glance at the flower-draped town of Dinkelsbühl and its Gothic church; then a plunge into history in medieval Rothenburg with its Renaissance town hall and Cathedral; a museum of crime; and half-timbered houses galore. You'll need a car.

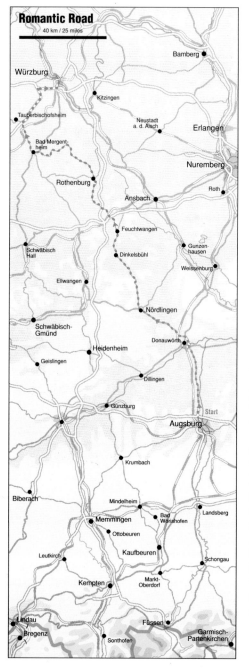

Romantic Road
40 km / 25 miles

It's hard to find anything much more romantic than the stretch of the Romantic Road between Nördlingen, Dinkelsbühl and Rothenburg ob der Tauber. North of Augsburg, the B25 affords glimpses of castle towers and church spires before leading you through 16th-century walled towns, their half-timbered facades laden with geraniums. But the drive is nothing compared to a walk around the towns themselves. A traveller with time to spare will want to tarry in each of the three mentioned above; if you have only a day, look at Dinkelsbühl in the morning, then go on to lovely Rothenburg. Be warned that this town, the undisputed pearl of the Romantic Road, is also its undisputed tourist attraction, extremely crowded on weekends and holidays.

Dinkelsbühl's picturesque main square is a feast for the eye. In summer, the house facades are buried in flowers; in winter, the snow-clad gables have the smug serenity of a Christmas card. Across from the red building of the tourist office, **St George's Cathedral** is a Gothic masterpiece with delicate clusters of pillars and jewel-like stained-glass

Flamboyant facade in Dinkelsbühl

windows. On the other side of Marktplatz is the **Deutsches Haus** (German House), built by the Drexler family in order to demonstrate their new status when they were elevated to the nobility in 1556. The six-storey, half-timbered house with its asymmetric facade today houses a restaurant.

Behind St George's, a narrow street leads to the **Wörnitz Gate** in the old city walls. These 14th-century fortifications were only preserved thanks to King Ludwig I, who intervened when the citizens began pulling them down to use the stone as building material in the 19th century. In front of the gateway, the lion on the medieval **Lion Fountain** displays his tongue in a threatening roar. Go through the gate and cross the footbridge for a look at the walls from the outside, mirrored in the calm water.

From here, a footpath follows the walls around to the left, where you can re-enter the city by way of the little street Badgässlein, coming out by the old Spital (home for the sick and elderly). Built in 1280, this rambling collection of buildings around a green, park-like yard still houses a home for old people, as well as the city's **Historical Museum**, its collection devoted to local lore and lifestyles through the ages, a concert hall and a public sauna: all in all, a remarkably successful integration of the historical into modern daily life.

Medieval Rothenburg

The Spital fronts on Dr-Martin-Luther-Strasse, which leads back to the centre of town. Up Steingasse to your right is the restaurant/hotel **Weisses Ross** (Steingasse 12, Tel: 09851-2274), which serves a very good lunch. This establishment's new annexe is located in an inventively converted stable; clean modern and luxurious rooms still display the heavy beams and dormer windows of the former farming facility.

Suitably refreshed and heading north from Dinkelsbühl on the B25, you'll pass the turn-off to another lovely romantic town, Feuchtwangen, on the hour-long drive to **Rothenburg ob der Tauber**. Perched high above ('ob') the Tauber river,

All roads lead to the Market Square

this enchanting town looks as if its 1274 city charter had been issued only yesterday; the sole indications of modernity are the tour buses parked outside the walls. Leave your car with the buses near **Galgentor** (Gallows Gate), part of the second, 14th-century ring of city defences. As you walk toward the city centre you'll pass through part of the earlier, 12th-century fortifications: the **Weisse Turm** (White Tower), near which a small garden lined with Jewish gravestones is dedicated to Rabbi Meir ben Baruch, a 13th-century Talmudic scholar.

All roads in Rothenburg lead to **Marktplatz** (Market Square). To your right, the 1446 tavern (built for the city councillors) features, on the outside, a double-faced clock from 1683 as well as a set of mechanical figures who enact the most famous incident of Rothenburg's history several times a day (hourly 11am–3pm and 8–10pm). During the Thirty Years' War, in 1631, General Tilly and his Catholic League troops were retreating through Protestant Rothenburg. Fearing certain destruction, the Mayor of Rothenburg, Nusch, made a bet with Tilly: if he could down the contents of a goblet filled with 3¼ litres of wine at one gulp, Tilly would spare his town. Tilly agreed, the mayor emptied the goblet and the rest is history.

Dominating the square is the Town Hall, its 1570s Renaissance facade built when a wing of the older, Gothic section of the building burnt down in 1501. The building's other original wing, built in the 13th and 14th centuries, fronts Herren-

Riemenschneider's Altar of the Holy Blood

gasse, on your left. With a height of 60m (200ft), the old tower offers a great view to anyone in excellent physical shape, but its narrow stairs are not for the faint-hearted.

Walk behind the square to the right to find the **St-Jakobs-Kirche** (Church of St James). This cream-coloured, 14th-century church gets so much light from its tall windows that even the

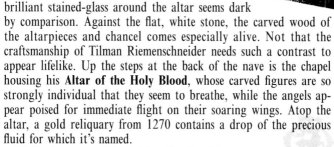

brilliant stained-glass around the altar seems dark by comparison. Against the flat, white stone, the carved wood of the altarpieces and chancel comes especially alive. Not that the craftsmanship of Tilman Riemenschneider needs such a contrast to appear lifelike. Up the steps at the back of the nave is the chapel housing his **Altar of the Holy Blood**, whose carved figures are so strongly individual that they seem to breathe, while the angels appear poised for immediate flight on their soaring wings. Atop the altar, a gold reliquary from 1270 contains a drop of the precious fluid for which it's named.

While almost equal in height, the church's two towers are quite different in appearance; legend has it that the southern tower was built by the master builder, and the northern one by his apprentice. Furious that his student's work was better than his own, the master flung himself from the southern tower to his death.

If you're ready for a break at this stage, the tree-shaded garden of the **Hotel Reichs-Küchenmeister** (Kirchplatz 8–10, Tel: 09861-2046) to your right, overlooking the back of the church, is a pleasant, if well-frequented, place to stop.

If you want to keep going, then Klingengasse leads right under the Holy Blood Chapel to **St Wolfgang**, surely one of the more unusual churches you'll encounter. This shepherds' church is built into the city walls; twisting staircases give access to the walls above (where, once you've passed through the low-ceilinged Shepherds' Dance Museum, you can see the 'Pitch-Face' (Pechnase) stone face through whose mouth hot pitch was poured down on would-be attackers) and the defensive underground passageways below. To the right of the main altar, the **Wendelin Altar**, which is dedicated to the shepherds' patron saint, has a shallow groove in the stone at the front where defenders of the town, called to arms, sharpened their swords while blessing them at the same time.

Leaving the church, bear right and walk outside the walls, looking down across the Tauber river at the funny little tower built as a weekend getaway by Rothenburg's most popular Mayor, Heinrich Toppler, in 1388. Ahead of you, on the narrow spur at the western extremity of the Old Town is the **Burggarten** (Castle Garden), occupying the site of the town's 10th-century castle, which was destroyed by an earthquake in 1356. From the green, shaded lawns you can look down and see the double-arched bridge over the Tauber built in the 14th century. Inside the **Burgtor** (Castle Gate), the first

Creatively carved timber

left leads to the **Burg Hotel** (Klostergasse 1–3, Tel: 09861-5037), whose gorgeous, individually-furnished rooms all command a piece of the view.

Running along the southern wall, Burggasse leads to the former monastery which houses Rothenburg's unique **Museum of Crime** (April–October 9.30am–6pm; November, January, February 2pm–4pm; December, March 10am–4pm). Devoted to instruments of torture and punishment through the ages, the museum is filled with exhibits carefully explained in both German and English, offering a diverting look at another side of daily life in the Middle Ages.

The Burgtor leads into the castle

Bustling Schmiedgasse leads, to the right, to Rothenburg's most popular (and most photographed) site, the **Plönlein**. This consists of a fork in the road leading to two of the city's hallmark gateways, separated by a half-timbered house. If you want to get away from the crowd, continue along the walls until you come to the **Spital**; here, you'll be left alone to investigate the lovely old buildings and the Gothic carvings of the tiny **Church of the Holy Ghost** in peace.

A fine dinner in the **Goldener Hirsch Hotel** (Untere Schmiedgasse 16–25, Tel: 09861-61372) will fortify body and soul after a long day of sightseeing.

9. Würzburg

A residence fit for a bishop; a bridge across the Main and the House of Franconian Wine; a mighty fortress; and dinner in a medieval flower garden.

Although it's been home to Bishops since the bishopric was established in 742, the Franconian city of **Würzburg** didn't have its true flowering until after the 16th century. Prince-Bishop Julius Echter of Mespelbrunn (1573–1617) founded the first University and the Juliusspital for the poor (but also encouraged witch-hunts and persecution of the Jews); the 17th and 18th centuries were dominated by the Schönborn family, patrons of the arts who oversaw the building of the Residence.

The stairwell of the Residenz

Liquid refreshment, as well as art, has its own flavour in this northernmost corner of Bavaria. As the south is famous for beer, Lower Franconia is famous for its wine, which comes in distinctive round bottles called *Bocksbeutel* (a vernacular term for the reproductive organs of goats).

The best place to start in Würzburg and the showpiece of the city is the Prince-Bishop's palatial **Residenz**. For years, the Prince-Bishops had lived in the fortress of Marienburg; but Johann

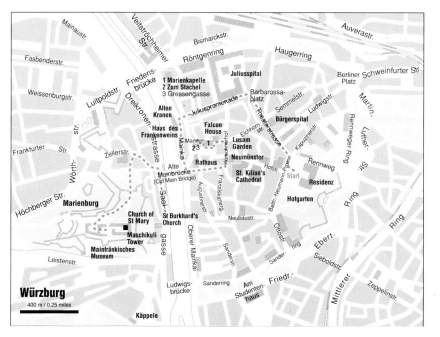

Würzburg
400 m / 0.25 miles

1 Marienkapelle
2 Zum Stachel
3 Gressengasse

Philipp Franz von Schönborn, who took office in 1714, wanted to be more in the centre of things, and commissioned 33-year-old Balthasar Neumann to build him a suitable abode. A host of builders and artists were drawn into the 25-year project, one of them responsible for the ceiling frescoes above the magnificent double staircase: Giovanni Battista Tiepolo. After visiting the interior (guided tours of the furnished rooms, including the Hofkirche, a Neumann jewel with Tiepolo trimming, April–September 9am–5pm, October–March 10am–4pm), walk through the Residence's wonderful formal gardens. If you're in the city in June, you may catch one of the torchlit outdoor performances of the annual **Mozart Festival**.

Walking up Theaterstrasse from the Residence, you'll come to the **Bürgerspital**, founded in 1319 and still in use both as a home for the poor and elderly and a wine-cellar where you can eat and drink well and inexpensively (Bürgerspital Weinstuben, Theaterstrasse 19, Tel: 0931-13861). Residents of the Bürgerspital still receive one free glass of wine every day as a part of their keep.

Turn left at Barbarossaplatz into the Juliuspromenade which runs by the **Juliusspital**, a palace built by Petrini after Julius's original

Cross the river to the Marienburg

1576 building burnt down in 1699. A rococo apothecary's is preserved on the ground floor; while, true to Spital tradition, there's a wine-cellar in the basement (Juliusspital Weinstuben, Juliuspromenade 19, Tel: 0931-54080). Straight ahead, you can see the **Alten Kranen**, the old crane on the river Main dating from 1773; next to it, at the **Haus des Frankenweins** (House of Franconian Wine, Kranenkai 1, Tel: 0931-12093), you can sample a variety of local vintages.

Proceed along the Mainkai to the picturesque **Alte Mainbrücke** (Old Main Bridge), with its statue of St Kilian. Cross the river here to come to the beginning of the steep path up to the fortress of **Marienburg**. Although the city has known defeat, the fortress, locals say, has never been taken by military force; treachery opened the gates to conquering Swedish troops in the Thirty Years' War. On the grassy slopes around the walls there's a monument to the Peasants' Revolt of 1525, in which the lower classes attempted to storm the fortress by burying explosives under its walls, an undertaking as bloody as it was futile.

Once you've climbed the path, commence your tour of the fortress with the **Mainfränkisches Museum** (open daily April–October 10am–5pm, November–March 10am–4pm), whose exhibits include

an amazing collection of statuary by local son Tilman Riemenschneider. Riemenschneider (1460–1531) was a highly regarded artist during his active career, so popular that he was elected Würzburg's Mayor in 1520; siding, however, with the peasants in the 1525 uprising, he was imprisoned and tortured, and never worked again. Politics and art don't mix.

Architectural testimonials from every era are present in the collection of buildings that comprises the fortress. Earliest of all is the **Church of St Mary** with its round chapel, dating from 704, at the centre of the main courtyard; the latest (excepting post-war reconstruction) is also round, Balthasar Neumann's 1728 **Maschikuli Tower** on the south side of the walls, facing Neumann's hillside chapel **Käppele** further upstream, a famous pilgrimage church devoted to the Holy Virgin. You can also see the Renaissance wellhouse, and the tower where Riemenschneider was held prisoner (guided tours April–September 9am–5pm, October–March 10am–4pm, closed Monday).

Once you've finished in the fortress, descend to the Saalgasse, which runs alongside the river Main past the home of the Fishermen's Guild (founded in 1010) on the left to **St Burkhard's Church**. The interior of this church includes 19th-century frescoes by the altar, Gothic choir stalls with marvellous angels' heads on the back, a Riemenschneider Madonna, and a long, chunky Romanesque nave with round arches.

Retrace your steps to recross the Old Main Bridge and pass the city's 12th-century **Rathaus** (Town Hall) and Sternplatz, once the heart of the tradesmens' district (as the names of surrounding streets like Doctor Street or Cobbler Street indicate), towards the Cathedral. **St Kilian's Cathedral** was another casualty of war; the reconstructed version gives an idea of its prototype and displays many of its original art treasures. Among these, of course, are

works by both Riemenschneider and Balthasar Neumann; Riemenschneider's memorial stone is also located in the Cathedral (or a copy of it; the original is in the museum), on the north wall. Examination reveals just how scarce funds were in this

The distinctive 'Bocksbeutel'

The Falcon House

once-prosperous family after the master's death: there was no money for a new stone for his son, and his father's had to do double duty with the addition of the younger man's name along the bottom when he died.

Up Kürschnerhof you can see the facade of the **Neumünster** on the right, which was 'baroque-ised' in 1720. Although the Würzburg Cathedral is dedicated to St Kilian, it's this church which was built over the saint's grave. There's another significant grave behind the church in peaceful **Lusam Garden**: that of medieval poet and troubadour Walther von der Vogelweide. His surname means 'bird-meadow', and the lid of his tomb contains four hollows for water for the birds.

The next turn on the left brings you to the yellow **Falcon House**, its stuccoed baroque facade exactly reconstructed after the 1751 original. Ahead of you, the tall late Gothic church is the 15th-century **Marienkapelle** (Mary's Chapel). Over its south door are copies of Riemenschneider's *Adam and Eve* (the originals are in the museum), while the north side door features an even more unusual ornament: faced with the challenge of physically depicting the Immaculate Conception, the sculptor showed God impregnating the Virgin by means of a tube running into her ear.

Down Marktgasse and left onto Gressengasse, and you'll arrive at **Zum Stachel** (Gressengasse 1, Tel: 0931-52770) in time for dinner. First mentioned in 1413, this famous restaurant was frequented by Riemenschneider and his cronies, and its proprietor hid peasants fleeing after the 1525 uprising. Its outdoor courtyard, an effusion of stone arches and geraniums, seems more like a stage set than a piece of history, but you can't go wrong here dining under the stars. Later on, you can walk past Riemenschneider's former residence at Franziskanergasse 1 (now the restaurant Pfeffermühle) on your way to the night spots that line Sanderstrasse.

A truly Immaculate Conception

FRANCONIA

Seeing the beauties of Würzburg may inspire you to explore more of the three provinces of Franconia (Franken). The name *Franken* actually dates back to 531, when the Frankish ruler Theodoric conquered the Thuringian empire and absorbed it into his own Frankish empire, *Frankenreich*. Comprising the northern section of Bavaria, Upper, Middle and Lower Franconia are regions with their own dialect, their own mores, even their own cuisine. The important and historic cities of Bamberg, Nuremberg and Bayreuth can all be easily reached by public transport. The following itineraries ensure you get a taste of the region's beautiful countryside as well by including a tour through the *Fränkische Schweiz* (Franconia's 'little Switzerland'), for which you'll need a car.

10. Bamberg

A medieval city which smokes its beer, has a town hall in the middle of its river, and boasts Germany's most marvellous cathedral.

Called the 'treasure chest of Franconia', Bamberg is an ideal city to use as a base while you explore this region. Gothic churches, baroque palaces, and half-timbered artisans' houses with 15th-century dates over their doorways all contribute to the city's visual charm, as do the flowering riverside balconies of the neighbourhood nicknamed 'Little Venice'. A seat of art and culture since its founding in 1007, and one of Germany's first printing centres, Bamberg has preserved this heritage with its university, theatre, and the Bamberg Symphony, widely known as one of Germany's finest orchestras. At night, people meet in the city's pubs for another local speciality, smoked beer (*Rauchbier*).

Bamberg's 'Little Venice'

If you've come by car, one of the city's many well-marked car parks is on Schillerplatz, the broad square where the **E.T.A. Hoffmann Theatre** is located. Author, playwright, and would-be composer, Hoffmann (1776–1822) was long a resident of Bamberg, employed by the city theatre; today, he's best known for his stories, familiar to many as *The Tales of Hoffmann*. The house where he lived for four years, **Schillerplatz 26**, is today a museum.

At the end of the square, follow Richard Wagner Strasse to Nonnenbruecke, then turn up Am Kanal. Before long, you'll sight the **Town Hall**, perched on an islet in the river Regnitz, its older, half-timbered section appended to a taller, baroque abdomen. Originally dating from 1461, the building was 'baroque-ised' in the 1700s; additions from this period include the tower and murals depicting classical heroes and significant Bambergers ensconced in flourishes of architectural *trompe l'oeil*.

For the best view of the Town Hall, cross the first bridge on your left before the building and stand on the tip of the island just across from it. As you face the Town Hall, **Geyersworth Castle** is right behind you. Now home to city administration offices, the medieval palace with its ivy-covered courtyard and

The Town Hall on the river

fountain was rebuilt in the 1500s by the Prince-Bishops, who lived there until the construction of the New Residence in 1697.

Return to Nonnenbruecke and cross the river to Concordiastrasse. A right will bring you to an uphill intersection and the yellow baroque facade of the **Böttinger House** (1707–13). As you begin the steep ascent on the street called Eisgrube, notice the doorknob on **house No 14**: a wizened, smiling face, polished by use over the years. This doorknob was immortalised in Hoffmann's story *The Golden Pot*, in which it began to speak to the protagonist as he moved to enter the building.

To the right, a flight of steps ascends to the 14-century Church of Our Lady, more commonly known as **Obere Pfarre** (Upper Parish Church), a Gothic wonder bearing the baroque traces of the 17th century. As the church's special religious festival is the Assumption of the Virgin, it's fitting that it owns a painting of this event by Tintoretto, hanging on the back wall of the right-hand

The talking doorknob

aisle. Even better is the 14th-century **Tabernacle**, in a chapel behind the high altar, carved with row upon row of figures depicting the Entombment of Christ, the Apostles, and the Last Judgment. Outside, a porch on the north side of the building depicts the Wise and Foolish Virgins (the wise ones appropriately self-righteous, the foolish ones with a slightly bovine air).

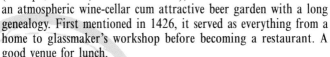

Down Unterkaulberg you will come to the little square **Pfahl-plätzchen** and the **Ring-Vogel-Haus** (Pfahlplätzchen 4, Tel: 0951-55080), an atmospheric wine-cellar cum attractive beer garden with a long genealogy. First mentioned in 1426, it served as everything from a home to glassmaker's workshop before becoming a restaurant. A good venue for lunch.

From here Judenstrasse runs into Karolinenstrasse, the last leg of the steep ascent to Bamberg's showpiece **Cathedral** (*Dom*). Built atop one of the city's seven hills and consecrated in 1012, this is one of the masterpieces of German sacred architecture. Its patron saints are Peter and George, but its interior is more markedly influenced by the ubiquitous sculptors Veit Stoss and Tilman Riemenschneider, the former with his dark wooden **Christmas Altar** in the left transept, and the latter with his **tomb of Heinrich and Kunigunde** (the city's patron saints and founders) at the centre of the Cathedral. Neither of these masters, however, was responsible for the most famous sculpture in the city: no one knows who created the ethereal **Bamberger Reiter**. Said by some to represent the ideal of Christian knights in the Middle Ages, this unknown and beautiful horseman sits his mount in a niche high above the ground, at the rear of the building.

Across from the Cathedral is the rambling **New Residence**, commissioned by the Bishop of Bamberg and Elector of Mainz, Lothar Franz von Schönborn, in 1697. Its splendid tapestries and furnishings are visible on tours (April–September 9am–noon and 1.30pm–5pm, October–March until 4pm). One highlight is the richly ornamented **Emperor's Room** (*Kaisersaal*), where the Bamberg Symphony sometimes gives candlelight concerts. Through the main archway is the **Rose Garden**, in summer a veritable blanket of flowers, commanding a panoramic view of the city from its outdoor café tables (Café Im Rosengarten, open May–October).

Next to the cathedral is the original imperial and bishop's palace, the **Old Court** (*Alte Hofhaltung*). The Renaissance **Ratstube** faces the square; through the gateway, the courtyard is wonderfully picturesque, with all the half-timbers, gables and flowers a photographer could desire. Formerly the seat of city government, the building now houses Bamberg's **History Museum**.

Another hill, another church: but the view alone makes the ascent up to the former Benedictine monastery of **St Michael's** worthwhile (go out the rear of the Alte Hofhaltung to Domstrasse, and keep going up). The abbey was founded in 1012, but today's buildings went up in the 17th and 18th centuries. Unusual features include a ceiling frescoed with the images of over 600 medicinal herbs, and the tomb of St Otto behind the high altar (some say that creeping through its small opening is a sure cure for either backache or lumbago). In the former brewery, the **Franconian Brewing Museum** (Thursday–Sunday 1pm–4pm) explores the history of monastic breweries, once a thriving industry, but crippled by the secularisation of 1803 (today, only a handful of establishments, such as Ettal in itinerary 3, continue the brewing tradition).

One landmark of the region isn't in Bamberg at all. Back in the car, follow Obere Königsstrasse to the B173 toward Lichtenfels. About 30km (18 miles) on is the turnoff to the **Vierzehnheiligen**, the church of Fourteen Saints, considered by some to be Balthasar

Inside the Vierzehnheiligen

Neumann's greatest work. Flecked with gold and blue, the scrolled white interior is built around a mammoth shrine, said to have miracle-working properties, with depictions of all 14 of the eponymous saints. But while the rich rococo ornamentation and frescoes are all magnificent, here Neumann's real achievement was in defining the interior space of the building in a series of interlocking ovals. The oval pattern, such a typical element of the baroque, thus becomes an integral part of the design both in a two- and three-dimensional plain. For this alone, the building is an absolute masterpiece.

If you intend to stay in the area for dinner, return to Bamberg for a taste of genuine local cuisine at the restaurant **Brudermühle** (Schranne 1, Tel: 0951-540091).

From the former Residence city and Wagner temple of Bayreuth, past caves, cliffs and castles to the mountaintop church of Gössweinstein, the towering rocks of Tüchersfeld, and the half-timbered houses of medieval Forchheim.

Lovers of music know **Bayreuth** as the site of the annual Richard Wagner summer opera festival, and the place where the eccentric composer made his home. But the small city had aspirations to cultural grandeur even before Wagner arrived in 1874. In 1731, Wilhelmine, favourite sister of Frederick the Great, married the Margrave of Bayreuth and set out to convert the town she saw as a 'dung heap' into a residence befitting her cosmopolitan tastes.

Coming up from the large car park behind the Stadthalle (which hosts concerts and theatrical events), you're right around the corner from the **Neues Schloss** (New Palace), one of Wilhelmine's last projects, built in 1755 (tours April–September 10–11.20am and 1.30–4.10pm; October–March until 2.50pm). The Margravine Wilhelmine's *tour de force* is located a little further down Ludwigstrasse, which becomes Opernstrasse: the **Markgräfisches Opernhaus** (Margrave's Opera House) is a three-tiered baroque extravaganza (tours April–September 9–11.30am and 1.30–4.30pm, October–March 10–11.30am and

Richard Wagner

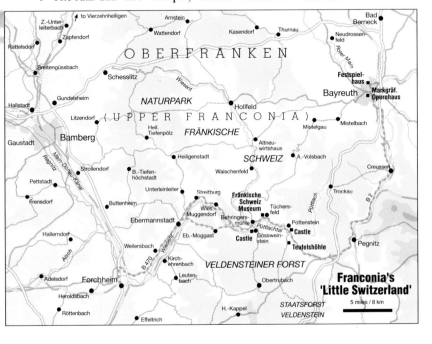

The Festspielhaus

1.30–3pm). The multi-faceted Margravine was herself a musician who played four instruments and composed an opera; she was also an avid student of philosophy, founding the *Friedrichsakademie* (destined to evolve into the University of Erlangen) in 1742.

Across from the theatre is the **Old Castle**, home to the margraves until 1754, reconstructed after 1945 bombings and today housing city administration offices. Behind the castle, you can rest your feet at an outdoor café before embarking on the 15-minute walk from Luitpoldplatz along Bahnhofstrasse to the **Festspielhaus** (Festival Theatre). Bayreuth's claim to international fame, this house, opened in 1876, is virtually a required sight for visitors to the area. Not that its plain brick exterior would in itself merit this kind of attention. Wagner wanted the focus of his theatre to be the events on stage, rather than the ornamentation – as anyone who's spent four hours sitting on one of the auditorium's bare wooden seats knows all too well. What was saved on decoration was put into the stage machinery, trail-blazing then and still remarkable today; the theatre's acoustics are also among the best in the world. Performances of Wagner's operas are given in August; tickets are almost impossible to get, but you can tour the theatre throughout the year (daily 10–10.45am and 2.15–3.45pm, October–March until 3pm).

If you're intrigued by the single-mindedness of a man who expected politicians to provide him with funds to indulge his creative desires, stop in at Wagner's home, **Haus Wahnfried** (1874), on your way back to your car. Located off Richard-Wagner-Strasse, the villa is today a Wagner Museum, filled with memorabilia (including the composer's piano) testifying to Wagner's eccentricities as well as his strengths. Recordings of the Wagner operas are played at 10am, 12pm, and 2pm.

Back in the car, follow the B2 south to the town of **Pegnitz**, renowned among international visitors principally for the luxurious **Pflaums Posthotel Pegnitz** (Nürnberger Strasse 12–16, Tel: 09241-7250). Its restaurant Pflaumengarten serves up *haute cuisine* interpretations of regional food; for a less expensive foray into fine Frankish fare, there's the Posthalterstube, also in the hotel.

From Pegnitz, the B470 leads straight through the heart of one of my favourite Bavarian regions: Franconia's **Little Switzerland**

The mill in Ebermannstadt

(*Fränkische Schweiz*), so called because of the resemblance which its rocky cliffs, vivid green hills and tumbling rivers bear to the original. In addition to some of Bavaria's most wonderful – and unusual – landscapes, the region is chock-a-block with castles, churches, and caves. In fact, the **Teufelshöhle** (Devil's Cave), on your left after about 9km (5 miles), is the largest cave in Germany – which won't come as a surprise once you see the yawning cave mouth on the other side of the river. This underground limestone labyrinth of glistening stalactites and stalagmites (the former, by the way, are the ones that hang from the ceiling; the latter, those that grow up from the ground) is open Easter to early November 9am–5pm, for 40-minute tours.

Nearby **Pottenstein** is overshadowed by an enormous cliff topped with dwellings. Just before you reach the village, a road on the right leads up to the **Burg** (Castle), originally dating from 918, and still inhabited today (visible on guided tours during the summer season). To see the village's historic centre, turn right on Forchheimer Strasse and park by the river to stroll along *Hauptstrasse* (main street) and the market place.

From Pottenstein, the B470 leads to **Tüchersfeld**. You'll see the remarkable cliff formations before you see the little town nestled beneath them: resembling some sort of giant mushroom growth, the rounded pillars of rock, crowned with flags and even a little house, tower spectacularly over the river valley below. Before you come to them, a road leads right to the **Fränkische Schweiz Museum**, devoted to the geology, culture, history, and Jewish heritage of the region (April–October Tuesday–Sunday 10am–5pm, November–March Sunday, Tuesday, Thursday 1pm–5pm). Opposite the museum turn-off, on an islet in the river Püttlach, is the half-timbered **Old Mill** (*Mühle*).

At the village of **Beringersmühle**, the three river valleys of the Fränkische Schweiz – the Wiesenttal, the Ailsbachtal, and the Püttlachtal – come together. From here, the car ascent to **Gössweinstein** is short but steep, rewarded by the sight of the yellow exterior of yet another fine building by Balthasar Neumann. Dedicated to (and named after) the shrine of the Holy Trinity which it houses, the **church**, begun in 1739, looks across the valley toward Gössweinstein's **Castle** (*Burg Gössweinstein*), first mentioned in the 11th century and ultimately

The cliffs at Tüchersfeld

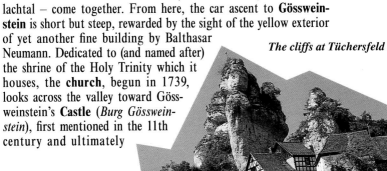

Flower lady in Forchheim

restored 100 years ago in a neo-Gothic style (daily April–October 10am–6pm).

From here, you can follow the river on the B470 past the towns of Muggendorf and Streitberg, both graced with castle ruins, or take a mountaintop short-cut through the farming village of Moggast: both routes lead through really beautiful countryside to **Ebermannstadt**, which is known as the capital of the *Fränkische Schweiz*, and whose marketplace is surrounded by beautiful half-timbered houses. Make sure you see the old water wheel on the river Wiesent. About 13km (8 miles) further on, the town of **Forchheim** is located on the western border of the region. Forchheim saw its glory days from the 9th to 11th centuries, when it was a major centre for the Carolingian dynasty, the site of royal elections and parliamentary assemblies – although you'd never know it to look at the beautiful, quiet little town it's become. Stop off at the city centre to see its half-timbered houses and **Town Hall** dating from the 1500s. Don't miss details like the whimsical relief figures on the **Magistrate's Building** of 1535, including a self-portrait of its creator, Hans Ruhalm.

12. Nuremberg

From the Holy Roman Empire to the '1000 Year Reich', from its glowering round towers to Germany's great National Museum, Nuremberg brings history soberly, thoughtfully, excitingly to life.

The heavy damage **Nuremberg** sustained in World War II was not inflicted for any reason other than that this medieval city was a symbol of the German spirit, so much so that Hitler had chosen it to be the rallying grounds for his '1000-year empire': this is also why it was chosen by the Allies as the site for the post-war Nazi trials. Notwithstanding, Nuremberg – which has existed

Medieval Nuremberg

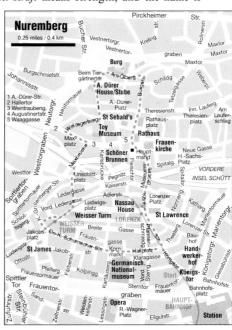

The Heilig-Geist-Spital on the Pegnitz

for more than 1000 years – does indeed represent some of what's finest about German culture. Today, carefully restored, Bavaria's second largest city has recovered its medieval air, complete with its skyline of round towers glowering above Gothic church spires, looking once again like the home of such artists of the Middle Ages and Renaissance as the poet Hans Sachs and the painter Albrecht Dürer.

Located on the A73 from Bamberg, the A3 from Würzburg, and the A9 from Munich, Nuremberg has so few places to park that you may want to consider arriving by train at the art nouveau railway station, which is an interesting sight in itself.

Enter the Old Town by way of Königsstrasse, past the threatening tower by **Königstor**, a reminder that city walls were originally designed to keep people out. Just inside the gateway to the left, you can see the **Handwerkerhof** (Artisans' Courtyard), a tourist-oriented marketplace with craft shops and eateries.

The **Church of St Lawrence**, straight ahead of you up Königsstrasse, was constructed between the 13th and 15th centuries. Looking down the centre aisle, your eye is trapped in a kind of visual web: move closer to free your view from the wire grill between you and the beautiful, floating carving of the **Annunciation** by Veit Stoss. To the left and rear is an equally airy work: the soaring **Tabernacle** of Adam Kraft. *Kraft* means strength, and the name is illustrated by the self-portrait of Kraft at the bottom of the piece; chisel in hand, he's supporting the whole thing on his shoulders. Across from the cathedral is the tower of the **Nassau House**, Nuremberg's oldest private residence.

Crossing the river Pegnitz, you'll see the arches of the **Heilig-Geist-Spital** leading over the river on your right. Another of Bavaria's wonderful medieval homes for the aged and sick, still in use today, the facility was founded in 1332 with

Albrecht Dürer self-portrait

private funds; in the 16th century, it was built out over the river simply because there was no more space to expand it on land.

From the Spital, it's not far to the marketplace, where the broad facade of the **Frauenkirche** (Church of Our Lady) stands guard over the striped awnings of vendors or, in December, the original Bavarian *Christkindlmarkt* (Christmas market). This tradition dates from Nuremberg's conversion to Protestantism in 1525; when Luther did away with the Catholic canon of saints, he replaced the gift-giving days of St Nicholas Day (6 December) and Epiphany (6 January) with Christmas Eve, when the Christ Child (*Christkind*) brought gifts to all. The markets have since spread through most of Catholic Bavaria, which conveniently ignores their Protestant roots in the interests of good business.

At one corner of the marketplace is the **Schöner Brunnen** (Beautiful Fountain), planned, like the rest of the square, under Emperor Charles IV; the fountain's forty figures range from Biblical prophets to King Arthur. Less attractive is the marketplace's history: it was built on the site of the Jewish quarter after it was levelled and its residents wiped out in 1349.

Rathausplatz runs between the 1340 **Rathaus** (Town Hall) and **St Sebald's**, one of Nuremberg's oldest churches, which contains the marvellous bronze **tomb of St Sebald** by Peter Vischer. To get from here to the **Burg**, or castle, which dominates the city, just walk toward the castle towers – uphill.

After around 1050, this castle, in various incarnations, kept Nuremberg an important centre for the Holy Roman Emperors for the next 500 years. Prominent here is the mighty **Sinwell Tower**; other features are the 50-m (164-ft) deep **Tiefer Brunnen** (Deep Well) and the double chapel, its upper level reserved for the Emperor and court, while the common people remained below (castle tours 9am–noon and 12.45–5pm, October–March 9.30am–noon and 12.45–4pm).

Walking down the street Am Ölberg from the castle will bring you to the square Beim Tiergärtnertor. Opposite half-timbered **Pilatus House** is the house where **Albrecht Dürer** lived for almost 20 years, today a small museum with furnished rooms and plenty of reproductions of Dürer's work (10am–5pm, Wednesday until 9pm, closed Monday; November, January and February 1–5pm). Albrecht-Dürer-Strasse is a quaint old street of shops and restaurants; stop off for lunch at number 6, the red-and-white half-timbered **Albrecht Dürer Stube** (Tel: 0911-227209).

Meander back through the city via **Weissgerbergasse** (one of Nuremberg's best-preserved old streets), down Maxplatz to the 15th-century house **Weinstadl**, then over the river at scenic **Maxbrücke**, from which you can see the oldest suspension bridge in Europe (1824) on your right. To the south, on Ludwigsplatz, the **Weißer Turm** (White Tower) is a remnant of the city's first, 13th-century fortifications; before it, the modern fountain **Ehekarussell** represents a rather free interpretation of Hans Sachs's 16th-century poem about the ups and downs of marriage.

If you're in a museum-going mood, spend the rest of your day in the **Germanische Nationalmuseum** on nearby Kornmarkt. Founded in 1852 and devoted to the history, art, culture and daily life of the German-speaking world from 30,000BC to the present, it's one of the biggest and best museums in Europe. An afternoon is time enough to take in part of the art gallery, or the furniture or toy collection, or one of the museum's temporary exhibits (Tuesday–Sunday 10am–5pm, Thursday until 9pm; English-language tours the first and third Sunday of each month).

If you'd rather miss the museum then take U-Bahn number 1 or 11 from the railway station one stop to Aufsessplatz and board tram 4 to Dutzendteich, at the edge of the **Nazi Rally Grounds** (*Reichsparteitagsgelände*), to see quite a different side of the city's past. Although the Nurembergers were not as a whole, in fact, very pro-Nazi in 1933, Hitler chose the city as the site for the annual Party Rally, and laid out the facilities on a typically grandiose scale. Many of the buildings have been left standing as a reminder of the past. Inside the **Zeppelin Tribune**, the exhibit **Faszination und Gewalt** ('Fascination and Power') explores the Nazi phenomenon (July–October Tuesday–Sunday 10am–6pm). There's also the Great Road, 60m (200ft) wide, and huge Congress Hall, never completed, by the Dutzendteich lake. The city has been at something of a loss to know what to do with some of these buildings; the grounds around them are, however, a lovely public park.

The castle at night

Lower Bavaria

Bavaria's two backwater provinces, the Upper Palatinate and Lower Bavaria (*Oberpfalz* and *Niederbayern*) are, in my opinion, two of its best. The country here includes the darkly beautiful Bavarian Forest, still with the feeling of wildness that more populous landscapes to the south have come to lack; while the cities – Regensburg, Passau and Landshut – haven't been fixed on the tourist map to the same degree as their westerly cousins. Travelling through the region means discovering hidden treasures. These provinces remain a well-kept secret; a visit here is highly recommended. The towns and cities can easily be reached by public transport, but for touring the Forest you're better off with a car.

Ferry across the Danube

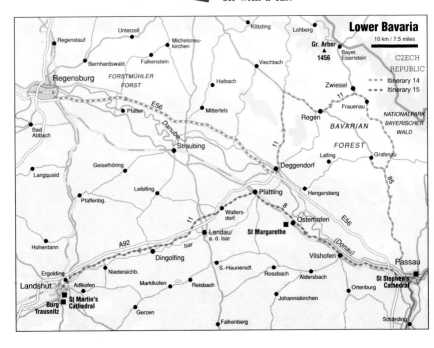

13. Regensburg

Untouched by war and off the main tourist map, the ancient Free City and seat of Imperial Diets has kept not only its sense of the past, but the actual buildings themselves, from Roman remains to a medieval restaurant which has been serving sausage ever since the 12th century.

One of the few Bavarian cities spared in World War II, **Regensburg** wears its age with a flair distinct from that of rebuilt cities like Nuremberg, Würzburg or Augsburg. Perhaps this is precisely because it was never reconstructed: the builders of this city approached it without the preconceptions of modern restorers trained to revere and duplicate the past. Here, what you get is pure history and Regensburg's streets and buildings are somehow severe, sober testimony to the fact the people who once dwelt here were a race considerably different from soft modern man.

The city sprawls around the focal point of its **Cathedral**, and, if its lacy towers weren't built until the 1860s, the dark interior is clearly of another age. From the arching blackness, brilliant stained glass bursts forth with a luminosity unequalled in all but a handful of great Gothic cathedrals (Chartres comes to mind; and Bishop Leo was, in fact, inspired by French models in

The Stone Bridge and the Cathedral

1275, bringing in a French builder when his own workers, used to the Romanesque style, had trouble achieving the effect he wanted). Priceless medieval treasures, manufactured in the glassworks of Zwiesel and other towns, the windows float free of the dark walls and hover overhead with their vibrant, coloured light. Beneath them is the shine of the High Altar, made of silver and copper by Regensburg artisans in the 18th century. When your eyes have adjusted to the darkness, you can make out sculpture and carvings like the Annunciation Angel and Mary, standing opposite each other on the two front columns of the nave, the angel smiling in childish, Gothic delight. Adjacent to the church is little **All Saints' Chapel**, even older than the Cathedral, with the faded remains of its original, 12th-century frescoes.

Outside and toward the back of the building is the **Diocesan Museum of St Ulrich's**, a creatively renovated church containing Gothic art treasures from throughout Bavaria.

The Historische Wurstküche

Go along Altdorferplatz until you come to the Alter Kornmarkt, the city grain market from the Middle Ages to the 19th century, bordered by some of Regensburg's oldest buildings. Legend links the **Alte Kapelle** (Old Chapel), to the south, with Emperor Constantine and the year 313, as well as with Agilolfing dukes in the 700s; it's certain that Ludwig the German had it renovated for his palace in 875, although the building's baroque-ised interior doesn't betray any such advanced age. On the north side, by the arch you came through, the doughty **Roman Tower** was not, in fact, a product of the Romans, but of Carolingian builders topped (literally) by 13th-century craftsmen.

If it's old you want, go to the church called **Niedermünster** (on the street of the same name). It may seem like just any other baroque church, but excavations here uncovered traces of Roman and Germanic buildings dating back to the 2nd century (the Germanic tribes were wont to give the Romans a hard time, destroying their camp a couple of times in the 3rd century); in the 8th century, a church was built to house the tomb of St Erhard, to be replaced, in the 12th century, by the present building. Further on, the same street leads to Unter den Schwibbögen, where, to the left, you can clearly see remains of the **castle** (*Castra Regina*) which the Romans founded in 179 (replacing the impermanent little camps which had gone before), including the clumsy, massive arch of **Porta Pretoria**, the riverfront gate through the walls.

From here walk down to the bank of the Danube, where you can see the **Steinerne Brücke** (Stone Bridge) arching over the river. This bridge seemed a miracle when it was built in 1135, the first stone bridge in Europe. The story goes that the engineer in charge made a pact with the Devil in order to complete it, promising him the own-

ers of the first eight legs across the bridge, and then foiling him by sending over a dog and two chickens. Before the bridge, built into the old city walls, is the modest **Historische Wurstküche** (Tel: 0941-59098), a Regensburg trademark, which allegedly began serving up its delicious, low-priced sausages for workers on the bridge in the 12th century.

Brückstrasse runs back into the city and to Goliathstrasse, where the **Goliath House** features a gigantic mural of David and Goliath, a kind of ornament common in the 16th century. As you walk down this street, you can see the tall **Golden Tower**, a 13th-century house, on Wahlenstrasse to your left. Just before you come to Rathaussplatz, you'll see the old corner building which houses the mini-restaurant **Dampfnudel-Ulli** (Watmarkt 4, Tel: 0941-53297), laden with all manner of Bavarian décor, an ideal place to sample the ultra-Bavarian speciality *Dampfnudel*.

Fronting Rathausplatz is the **Altes Rathaus** (Old Town Hall), medieval in aspect, complete with drunkenly leaning walls and sloping stairs. Buy tickets in the tourist office on the ground floor for tours of the **Reichstagsmuseum** (English tours at 3.15pm), where you can see everything from council to torture chambers and learn quite a bit about the history of this city-state, which hosted Imperial Diets, or councils (Reichstag), from the 1600s to the 1800s.

From here, make your way down Untere Bachgasse to **St Emmeram's Church**. Yet another claimant to the title of 'Oldest Church in Regensburg', St Emmeram's was also formerly a monastery which, in the early Middle Ages, was the most important in all Bavaria. Begun in the 8th century, the church reflects changing architectural tastes through the ages, notably the cloisters (11th–14th centuries) and, predictably, a baroque interior by the Asam brothers.

When secularisation closed the monasteries in 1806, the adjoining *Kloster* came into the possession of the Counts of Thurn und Taxis, an aristocratic family which made its fortune with a monopoly on the postal service dating back to the 16th century. As soon as they obtained it, the Princes set about turning the monastery into a magnificent palace, which, still inhabited, is open for tours (Monday, Wednesday–Saturday 2pm and 3.15pm; Sunday and holidays 10.40am and 11.15am).

Danube illuminations

14. The Bavarian Forest and Passau

Watch vases being blown by the glassmakers of Zwiesel; then drive through the countryside of the Bavarian Forest to one of the loveliest places in Germany, the 'three-river city' of Passau.

Between Regensburg and Passau, the meandering Danube river (Donau) forms the southern border of one of Bavaria's less-known wonders: the **Bavarian Forest** (*Bayerischer Wald*). Lying between the Danube and the Czech border, this mountainous region is still off the beaten track – in part because its landscapes, which would be a major attraction in any other country, are overshadowed, in Bavaria, by the Alps. The area has thus remained the province of German holiday-makers who know a good thing in their own country when they see it.

Deep in the forest

The little town of **Zwiesel** (*Autobahn* from Regensburg to Deggendorf, then north on the B11 via Regen) lies only a few kilometres from the border of the Czech Republic. And it isn't only landscape which the region has in common with Czech Bohemia. Minerals in the soil are partly responsible for the fame of Bohemian glass throughout the world, and the drawing of a border didn't prevent the glassmaker's art from flourishing wherever this fertile ground was to be found.

Most of Zwiesel's innumerable **glass workshops** offer tours of the premises, allowing you to watch the painstaking processes by which glass is blown, cut, and even painted with delicate floral designs. Although tours are given only at fixed times, each manufacturer has an outlet which observes normal business hours (usually 9am–6pm, Saturday until 2pm); some of these are even open on Sunday, quite a rarity in Germany.

The workshops of **Ambiente** (Frauenauer Strasse 110; left off the ring road around the town, then left again) retain a rustic air, and the glassware they produce has a distinctive hand-blown quality (tours Monday–Friday 10am–2pm, Saturday until 1pm). An equally rustic product is to be found at the nearby **Bärwurzerei Hieke** distillery, Frauenauerstrasse 82 (for guided tours call 09922-1515). *Bärwurz* is the signature *digestif* of the Bavarian Forest, distilled from a special blend of local herbs; the tasting session offered on these premises should separate *Bärwurz* fans from foes.

Continue up the ring road to **Theresienthal**, where you can see the more polished, packed-for-export products of **Schott** glassworks, or visit the **Theresienthal** glass workshop next door (Tuesday–Thursday 10am, 11am, 1pm; Monday and Friday 10 and 11am; Saturday 9.30am–noon). The complex of buildings in Theresienthal also includes the **Glass Museum** (10am–2pm) and **Theresienhof** (Tel: 09922-6255), a rustic restaurant with regional specialities. Outdoorsmen can pick up tips from the **National Park's Information Centre**, also located here.

From Zwiesel, take roads to Frauenau and Grafenau. With the sharp green of the meadows framed by sombre-toned evergreens, the landscapes here, particularly on a misty day, retain the feeling of the Old Germany depicted in fairy tales and storybooks. **Grafenau** is the centre of the **Bavarian Forest National Park**. Stop here if you have time, and follow the trails of the wild animal preserve, a sanctuary for bears, European bison, lynxes and wild boar. From Grafenau, the B85 leads down to the Danube (Donau); suddenly, you're driving along a road with cliffs above you, a river below, and, over the bridge ahead of you to your right, the other-worldly, truly enchanting city of Passau.

Sitting on today's Austrian border in a far corner of Germany, **Passau** was a stronghold and urban centre for Celtic, Roman and medieval civilisations. An independent principality from 1217–1803, and a major force in the Holy Roman Empire of the 13th century, its power waned in the shadow of Austro-Hungary, and Napoleon,

An aerial view of Passau

Typical 'Tracht'

finally, appended it to Bavaria. At the confluence of three rivers, it at least managed to maintain economic importance as a shipping centre: goods from the Inn river were loaded onto Danube barges to travel to Vienna or Budapest. Today, although the Rhine-Main-Danube canal, a massive project undertaken in 1921 to link the North Sea to the Black and finally opened in the autumn of 1992, may mean a revival of shipping trade, the main water traffic around Passau is passenger ships loaded with sightseers. Politically, the town is renowned as a bastion of arch-conservatism, as illustrated by the recent successful film *The Nasty Girl* (*Das Schreckliche Mädchen*), which delves into the local Nazi past. Nonetheless, it's a sleepy, watery, magical town, Germany's answer to Venice with its old houses (the buildings with the wilted air of fading roses), baroque architecture, and the brightness, even on grey days, that comes from light reflected off broad surfaces of water.

Built on a narrow spit of land, the small city is ideally suited to pedestrians; leave your car in one of the car parks (there are several near the bridge from the B85) before walking along the Danube and up Rindermarkt. To the right, Luragogasse leads to Domplatz and **St Stephen's Cathedral**. Passau, seat of the bishopric since 789, saw churches on this site in the days of the Romans; today's baroque cathedral was built when an earlier, Gothic building burned in the city fire of 1662. Huge and solid, ornate with white stucco figures like icing on a wedding cake, the building houses the largest organ in the world, with over 17,000 pipes. Noon concerts are given on weekdays from May to October.

The largest organ in the world

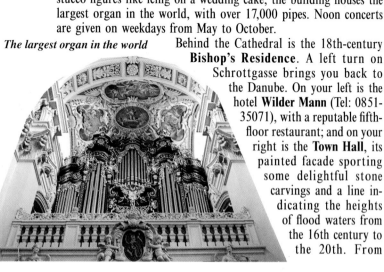

Behind the Cathedral is the 18th-century **Bishop's Residence**. A left turn on Schrottgasse brings you back to the Danube. On your left is the hotel **Wilder Mann** (Tel: 0851-35071), with a reputable fifth-floor restaurant; and on your right is the **Town Hall**, its painted facade sporting some delightful stone carvings and a line indicating the heights of flood waters from the 16th century to the 20th. From here, you should take the shuttle bus that runs half-hourly (11.30am–5pm) to the hilltop castle **Veste Oberhaus** across the river. The castle (Tuesday–Sunday 9am–5pm, closed February) has proved itself many times as a defensive outpost since it was begun in 1219; Napoleon even used it in 1805. Inside, the **City Museum** displays armour and costumes, a smithy, and a 14th-century chapel, while there's an impressive view of the city and rivers below.

Walking along the Danube towards the end of the Passau peninsula, you'll pass row upon row of tour boats offering a range of cruises – everything from the scenic cliffs of the Donaudurchbruch (Danube Gap) near Regensburg to longer jaunts down-river to Vienna. From the tip of the peninsula, dubbed **Three-River Corner** (*Dreiflußeck*), you have a view of all of Passau's rivers: on your left, the narrow Ilz emerges from the Bavarian Forest to meet the Danube; on your right, the Inn leads up from the south. Each of the rivers is a different colour, and the Inn's chalky and the Ilz's dark waters contrast clearly with those of the green, beautiful not-so-blue Danube.

From the Inn Promenade, a pedestrian bridge (past the road bridge) leads left over the river to a relic of Passau's more distant past, **St Severin's church**. Severin himself saw this church built before he died in 482; it was expanded in the 10th century, and newly renovated – so to speak – in 1497. Its white interior has the cleanness of old bones, speaking of a past so distant it's hard to comprehend.

Passau from the river

Leaving the church and passing under an arch in the medieval town wall, follow Am Severinstor to the **Roman Museum** (March–November Tuesday–Sunday 10am–noon and 2–4pm), located on the site where excavators uncovered remains of the Roman castle *Boiotro*. The Romans' bridge across the Inn was near here; today, you'll have to use the pedestrian bridge to return to the city centre and the restaurants Wilder Mann mentioned earlier or **Weisser Hase** (Ludwigstrasse 23, Tel: 0851-34066) for dinner.

15. Landshut

Along the Danube to Osterhofen and one of Bavaria's hidden baroque treasures. On to the river city of Landshut, capital of Lower Bavaria, with its brick Cathedral, castle, and ducal residence in German and Italian style.

The Asamkirche

Until the beginning of the 1980s, the narrow B8 along the Danube was the only access road to and from Passau – and what with ice in the winter, constant heavy traffic, and the occasional flood, it wasn't much fun to drive. The advent of the *Autobahn* along the other side of the river changed all that, and now the B8 can be seen for what it is: a pleasant riverside road through the pastel-lit scenery of the Danube valley, with the blue hills of the Bavarian Forest in the distance.

After about three-quarters of an hour from Passau, you'll get to **Osterhofen**: turn left at the traffic light toward Altenmarkt, and follow signs to the Asamkirche. Here, in the heart of Lower Bavaria, is one of the Asam brothers' greatest masterpieces: St **Margarethe**. Elaborate baroque flourishes and frescoes are so well harmonised that the church seems, quite simply, a spectacular whole. Its location also sets it off: that a farming community matter-of-factly attends Mass in this museum piece of a building illustrates the way Bavaria's artistic heritage is kept vividly, even startlingly, alive.

Continue on the B8 to Plattling, then follow signs to Wallersdorf and get on the B11 along the river Isar to **Landshut**. The skyline is recognisable by two towers: Trausnitz Castle, perched on a rise over the town, and the spire of St Martin's Cathedral, the tallest brick tower in the world at 131m (430ft). Drive right through town (left at the railway station down Luitpoldstrasse, and over the river) and park by the Isar in the big car park off Wittstrasse, from which it's only a short walk to the city centre.

Founded in 1204, a Wittelsbach capital on and off for the ensuing centuries, and now capital of Lower Bavaria, Landshut presents much of the aspect of a busy old market town which it must have displayed in the 1600s. Its main street, **Altstadt** (Old Town), is essentially a wide square surrounded with the kind of gabled houses familiar from Northern Renaissance painting; yet, filled with the hustle and bustle of modern life (shoppers hunting bargains, young people hanging out in front of McDonalds), it seems successfully to have made the transition to the present, rather than remaining tied, museum-like, to its past.

The most striking monument on this street is, of course, **St Martin's Cathedral** and its aforementioned tower, all built entirely of

74

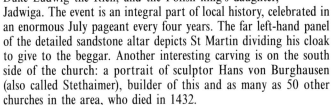

The Landshut Wedding procession

brick. Inside and out, brightly painted terracotta figures ornament portals and pillars; more recent stained glass includes, in the right aisle, a depiction of the **Landshuter Hochzeit**, the famous wedding that took place in 1475 between George, the son of Duke Ludwig the Rich, and the Polish king's daughter, Jadwiga. The event is an integral part of local history, celebrated in an enormous July pageant every four years. The far left-hand panel of the detailed sandstone altar depicts St Martin dividing his cloak to give to the beggar. Another interesting carving is on the south side of the church: a portrait of sculptor Hans von Burghausen (also called Stethaimer), builder of this and as many as 50 other churches in the area, who died in 1432.

Cross Altstadt to come to Landgasse and the **Vitztumb**, a building that served as Residence to the three last Dukes of Lower Bavaria (Ludwig the Rich, fat and gouty, died here in 1479), and later contained administrative offices. The restaurant **Beim Vitztumb** (Tel: 0871-22196) is another piece of Old Bavaria.

But this old building wasn't enough for Ludwig X. Second son of Duke Albrecht IV, the man who instituted the law of primogeniture, Ludwig insisted that, as the law was passed after his birth, he still had the right to half the duchy of Bavaria; accordingly, he governed in Landshut while big brother Wilhelm reigned in Munich. Nor was Trausnitz Castle up to Ludwig's standards; city residences were all the rage in the 1500s, and he accordingly started his own **Residenz** on Altstadt in 1530. The typical German palace facing the street is joined to a very Italianate arcade and wing; a trip to the court of Mantua in 1537 so inspired Ludwig that he had

the rest of his Residence built in the Italian style. He didn't have much time to enjoy it, dying in 1545, two years after its completion. (Tours April–September 9am–noon and 1–4.30pm (last tour); October–March until 3.30pm; closed Monday.)

Across from the Residence is the gabled Renaissance **Rathaus** (Town Hall); inside, frescoes depict the famous wedding. Further down the street, Altstadt 362 belongs to one of Landshut's breweries, Koller-Fleischmann, and houses both the comfortable **Café Woch'nblatt** and the disco **Bauhaus** (open after 9pm).

A juxtaposition of styles

The mighty Trausnitz Castle

Follow Rosengasse right from Altstadt to **Neustadt**; the 'new' in this broad street's name is somewhat misleading, as it was laid out in 1300. From here, Regierungsstrasse leads off to the former **Dominican monastery** which has housed the government (*Regierung*) of Lower Bavaria since 1839; adjacent to this is the green facade of a rococo church. Before you reach the building, Kramergasse, on the right, leads to the rectangular square **Freyung** dominated by the towers of **St Jodok** at one end. This square is the site of seasonal open-air markets such as the ceramics market; Landshut is, in fact, a centre for this craft, with one of Bavaria's only ceramics schools.

From Freyung, follow Kolpingstrasse to the **Hofgarten** (Court Garden), one of Bavaria's oldest and largest, its footpaths leading to scenic overlooks of the city on the way to **Burg Trausnitz** (Trausnitz Castle), an occasional residence of Wittelsbach dukes since 1204, expanded and reworked over the years (Duke Wilhelm IV followed Uncle Ludwig's penchant for the Italian Renaissance in his alterations of 1568), and, after all that, damaged heavily by fire in 1961. You can still see **St George's Chapel** and the distinctive **Narrentreppe** ('Fools' Staircase'), frescoed in 1578 with huge Commedia dell'Arte figures; perhaps even better is the view over the city from the castle's high balcony. When you descend from the heights, wander along the river, where the city's old buildings are reflected in the water and cafés and eateries like **Isar Klause** (Tel: 0871-23100) fill with relaxed drinkers and diners until nightfall.

Down by the river

Shopping

Mention Bavaria and many non-Germans will immediately think of *Lederhosen*, hats with 'shaving brushes' (usually made out of a tuft of chamois hair) and beer mugs. It's true that these items are readily available in the shops – and at far higher prices than one might have expected – but the discriminating shopper, whether hunting for an inexpensive souvenir or a valuable memento, will be able to find more distinctive, individual Bavarian objects. And shopping in Bavaria certainly isn't limited to local handicrafts. Cities like Munich offer a full range of international, cosmopolitan fashions, in clothing, furniture, books, and what-have-you.

Folk Crafts

Tracht, the folkloric costumes sported by locals at Oktoberfest or village fairs, is more than just a quaint affectation, as the unwitting shopper will be quick to discover from the pricetags on the *Lederhosen* or particularly the *Dirndl* (dress) of choice. First of all, these outfits signal the region from which the wearer hails. People who see their folk outfit as a reflection of their cultural heritage and identity are more than willing to pay for the skilled hand labour that goes into assembling one of these complicated ensembles.

Pottery for sale

Those who don't want a complete outfit can still invest in one of the *Tracht* accessories, such as a hat or fringed shawl. Munich's **Loden-Frey** (Maffeistrasse 7–9) and **Wallach** (Residenzstrasse 3), both in the city centre, are two of that city's finest outlets; Wallach also offers a range of Bavarian handicrafts.

Another major artisan industry is carved wood, a particular speciality of Upper Bavaria. From simple cutting boards to painted Madonnas and detailed Nativity scenes, you'll find it in the *Holzschnitzereien* (woodcarvers) and *Holzläden* (wood shops) of Munich

Wood carvings come in all shapes and sizes

and the Alpine foothills. Oberammergau is a notable centre for the craft: its streets are lined with shop windows filled with assemblages of carved and painted figures. In some rural shops, such as the *Holzschnitzerei* on Linderhoferstrasse 29, in Graswang, you may be able to see the master carvers at work; on the other hand, city shops, such as Munich's **Leute Holzwaren** (Viktualienmarkt 15), tend to have wider selections, including functional, not merely decorative, wooden items. In December, Munich or Nuremberg are the places to be if you're shopping for a Nativity scene: artisans come to the Christmas markets from throughout Bavaria. Although complete scenes are very expensive, individual figures can also be purchased.

Pewter (*Zinn*) objects – candlesticks and Christmas ornaments, serving dishes and soldiers – are sold at *Zinngiessereien* all over Bavaria; for a sampling, look in at **Mory Zinngiesserei** in the Munich Town Hall building, or **Antonie Kaiser**, behind the church of St Peter. In Passau, **Bauernkammel** (Steinweg 2) offers a variety of trinkets, most of them pewter. Bavarian ceramics also have a distinctive look: a ceramic 'bread pot' (*Brottopf*), rather than a bread box, can be found in nearly every Bavarian home. Landshut is home to an official school of ceramics; every September, the city hosts a three-day market, the **Haferlmarkt**, which attracts dozens of exhibitors. In Munich, the **Münchner Puppenstube** (Maxburgstrasse 4), which has a range of local crafts, carries a nice selection of ceramics. Available in ceramic, pewter or glass are the traditional beer mugs, called *Masskrug* in German.

An optical display

Folk crafts are also sold in departments of the major retail outlets of most Bavarian cities. Most Bavarian – indeed, German – cities have a branch of **Hertie**, **Karstadt**, or **Kaufhof**, which sell everything from *Tracht* to *Mode* (fashion), electronics (*Elektrogeräte*) to pantyhose (*Strumpf*). If it's German high fashion you want, there

are always outlets such as Margarethe Ley's **Escada** and **Laurèl**, with outlets in many cities, or the struggling, but Bavarian, **Sonia Bogner** in Munich (Residenzstrasse 2). A department store to end all department stores, filled with local colour, is Munich's **Ludwig Beck am Rathauseck**, on Marienplatz, which has designer fashions, Bavarian specialities, and, at Christmastime, in-house artisans working on their crafts. Also in Munich is **Radspieler**, on Residenzstrasse 23, its three floors crammed with an eclectic mix of art supplies, kitchenware, leather goods, and clothing.

Glass and China

Serious collectors and brides-to-be should head for the Bavarian Forest to stock up on their table settings and trousseau. Zwiesel and the surrounding area is filled with glass retail outlets (*see Day 14*), while the Upper Palatinate (Oberpfalz) to the north and east is rife with factory outlets selling name-brand goods at very good prices. About 45km (28 miles) north of Regensburg, the towns of Weiden and Neustadt an der Waldnaab contain legion crystal factory outlets, such as **Nachtmann Bleikristall** (lead crystal) (Tel: 09602-30176) and **Glas von Marion** (Tel: 09602-7462), both in Neustadt. Farther north, in Mitterteich, is the **Mitterteich Porcelain Factory Outlet** (Tel: 09633-300). More centrally located is Munich's **Nymphenburg Porcelain** factory, with showrooms in the Northern Schloss Rondell at Nymphenburg Palace and a store on Odeonsplatz.

Wines, Liqueurs and Delicatessen

It may be a bit much to ship home a crate of Bavarian beer, but a bottle of Franconian wine isn't difficult to transport. Famous for its dry white wines, Würzburg has plenty of purveyors of the local vintages, such as the Spitals or the **Haus des Frankenweins** on the river Main. Many parts of Bavaria have typical liqueurs which also make distinctive and unusual souvenirs. In the Bavarian Forest, it's *Bärwurz*; the Alps have *Enzian*, made from gentian root. Some monasteries and convents, like **Kloster Ettal** or **Frauenchiemsee**, continue to distill their own traditional blends.

In Munich there is a wide choice of delicatessens. Situated behind the Town Hall, **Dallmayr** is a veritable temple of fine food and drink, selling both international and regional specialities.

Carnival masks from the baker

Bavarian cuisine is either hearty or heavy, depending on your appetite and your mood. Main dishes are almost without exception based on pork, potato, and cabbage products; other vegetables are rare. To a traveller, the advantage of this kind of rustic cuisine is that you can discover marvellous meals in a tiny village *Lokal*: in Bavaria, good cooking is not the province of cities. There is also the choice offered by international restaurants – mostly Greek and Italian – even in the smallest of country towns.

A hallmark of the Bavarian diet is sausage (*Wurst*), displayed in the windows of butchers' shops (*Metzgereien*) in a mind-boggling range of sizes and varieties (a Berchtesgaden butcher even advertises *Touristenwurst*; one only hopes, in the town's summer crowds, that this is sausage *for* tourists, not, as the name might suggest, made of). Munich's particular speciality is *Weisswurst*, a light, white veal sausage flecked with parsley. A veritable religion has sprung up around these: they must be simmered, never boiled; served in a tureen of hot water; peeled before eating; dolloped with a particular kind of dark, sweet, grainy mustard (many restaurants have their own recipes) – and all this at mid-morning, the traditional time for the 'Weisswurst break'. Regardless of the early hour, the only possible beverage to accompany this snack is beer – *Weissbier* (a cloudy, yeasty brew with a distinctive flavour) at that.

Long red and brown *Bratwürste* (fried sausage) are common throughout the German-speaking world; but another distinctly Bavarian variety is the small, delicious, *Nürnberger Bratwurst*, usually served in sixes on a bed of *Sauerkraut*. In Franconia the sausages of choice are *Blaue Zipfel*, thin, tangy sausages in a vinegary brine, named for their slightly bluish grey hue. On the dinner table, *Wurst* only appear in groups; a *Wursteller* (platter) will include several different varieties. Don't confuse this with a *Schlachtteller* ('slaughter platter'), an arrangement of fresh blood and liver sausage together with pieces of boiled pork and kidney.

Another speciality is the ubiquitous *Leberkäse* (literally, 'liver-cheese'), a unique kind of meat loaf which languishes under heat

Schweinebraten mit Semmelknödel

lamps in every snack bar (*Imbissstube*) in Upper Bavaria; slabs of it are smeared with mustard and served in a *Semmel* (roll) for eaters on the go. However, when homemade in a country butcher's, fried on both sides and served with fried eggs and potatoes, it can be very tasty indeed. Mention should also be made of the distinctive Upper Bavarian *Saure Lüngerl*, lung prepared specially in a vinegar sauce.

A stand-by of every Bavarian restaurant is *Schweinebraten mit Blaukraut und Knödel* – roast pork with red cabbage and dumpling. Dumplings come in two varieties: *Semmelknödel*, made of rolls, and *Kartoffelknödel*, made of grated potatoes. For real pork fans, *Schweinshax'n* – pork knuckles – are as Bavarian as it gets. Repellent to some, delicious to others, they arrive encased in an armour of crisp skin and bubbling fat.

There are also options for non-meat eaters. *Rahmchampignons* (or *Pilze*) *mit Semmelknödel* are mushrooms in a cream sauce poured over a huge dumpling, which make a filling meal. Imported from Baden in the west and taken over by the Swabians, *Kässpätzle* can be found on most menus: this is a kind of homemade pasta with melted cheese and onion.

Beer gardens have their own specialities. You'll find *Hax'n* aplenty, as well as roast chicken (*Hendl*); *Rippchen*, spare ribs, are also popular. Giant pretzels (*Brez'n*) are a treat; if you want to be really Bavarian, smear them with *Obazda*, an orangey cheese spread made with camembert, butter, paprika and onion. You may notice people eating something that looks like paper: these are *Radi*, thinly sliced white radishes. To enjoy these properly, salt them and let them sit a few minutes until the salt is absorbed.

Beer, of course, is a favourite beverage; but you have to decide whether you want blond beer (*Helles*) or dark (*Dunkles*), yeasty, wheaty *Weissbier*, or even *dunkles Weissbier*. Then there's *Starkbier* in March, and *Wiesnbier* at the Oktoberfest, and, in Bamberg, *Rauchbier*... After all this, you may want to settle for *alkoholfreies Bier*, that is if you don't opt for the local shandy known as *Radler* (named after the Bavarian word for cyclist). If you don't drink beer at all, the only way to get a decent amount of liquid in a restaurant is to order a *Spezi* (half cola, half orange soda) or an *Apfelschorle* (half apple juice, half mineral water).

The word *Restaurant* works in most languages, but you may not find one of these in a small town: the word in German denotes something a bit more upmarket than it does in English. The general term for eateries is *Gaststätten*: this covers everything from fine dining to the corner pub (*Kneipe*, or *Lokal*). *Konditoreien* serve cake and coffee, as well, sometimes, as light meals; for *Wurst* and sandwiches, there's the corner *Schnellimbiss* (snack bar).

Munich

WEISSES BRAUHAUS
Im Tal 10
Tel: 089-299875
A venerable establishment whose decor is as authentically Bavarian as the *Schweinshax'n* and *Knödel* it serves. True Münchners come here at 11am to eat *Weisswurst*, a speciality of the city. Visitors should treat the strong dark *Weissbier* with respect.

Füssen

ZUM SCHWANEN
Brotmarkt 4
Tel: 08362-6174
Located in a building dating from the 15th century and serving elegant, yet still very Bavarian, cuisine (the changing daily menu is well worth sampling).

TIROLER WEINSTUBE
Franziskanergasse 1
Tel: 08362-6259
Serves hearty, tasty, inexpensive meals in its rustic upstairs dining room. The selection is not broad but dependable; you can eat at wooden tables in the company of a few locals.

Oberammergau

GRÖBL-ALM
On the B23 between Linderhof and Graswang
Tel: 08822-6434
A fine place to go for a hearty Bavar-

Weisswurst is eaten in the morning

Lunchtime

ian lunch while looking down over the green valley and the Alps. Meals include venison (*Wild*) with cranberries (*Preiselbeeren*), which in good weather can be eaten at one of the shaded tables on the outdoor terrace.

EIBSEE HOTEL
On Lake Eibsee
Tel: 08821-8081
With its lakeside balcony commanding a marvellous view of the Zugspitze, this restaurant offers fine dining. The cuisine reflects a French influence, although the menu includes the requisite Bavarian *Wurst* and cheese, spruced up a little to match the surroundings. The fresh grilled trout (*Forelle*) is especially delicious.

Mittenwald

ALPENROSE
Obermarkt 1
Tel: 08823-5055
One of Mittenwald's oldest, and most atmospheric, restaurants. Try something traditional like liver dumpling soup (*Leberknödelsuppe*) followed by *Schweinebraten mit Blaukraut* or, if you want something lighter, a plate of *Käsespätzle*. Live music on some evenings.

Chiemsee

GASTHOF INSELWIRT
Frauenchiemsee
Tel: 08054-630
A traditional eatery with a large terrace overlooking the water that tends

to be crowded with *Wurst-* and *Schwein-*hungry visitors.

Berchtesgaden

HOTEL-GASTHOF NUTZKASER
Just off the B305 from Berchtesgaden to Ramsau (signs to Hochschwarzeck)
Tel: 08657-388
A family-run establishment perched on a steep hillside, where you can eat your fill of hearty Bavarian fare in full sight of the Alps.

Augsburg

FUGGEREI-STUBE
Jakoberstrasse 26
Tel: 0821-30870
Specialities include a plate of *Wurst*, *Rahmchampignons mit Semmelknödel* and a selection of local Augsburg beers.

KÖNIG VON FLANDERN BRAUEREI
Karolinenstrasse 12
Tel: 0821-158050
An increasingly popular basement hang-out which serves only varieties of its own in-house brew, as well as light meals and snacks.

Dinkelsbühl

WEISSES ROSS
Steingasse 12
Tel: 09851-2274
This acclaimed restaurant is sometimes booked for businessmen attending seminars and conferences. Be that as it may, its updated versions of a variety of traditional dishes are well worth sampling.

Rothenburg

HOTEL REICHS-KÜCHENMEISTER
Kirchplatz 8-10
Tel: 09861-2046
A pleasant, if well-frequented, place to stop, offering all the standard German dishes to a predominantly tourist clientele.

GOLDENER HIRSCH HOTEL
Untere Schmiedgasse 16-25
Tel: 09861-61372
This restaurant is a little too well-known for its own good, but offers meals that are a cut above most tourist fare, even if a bit pricey. There are a variety of dining areas, including an outdoor terrace with a lovely view of the town.

Würzburg

BÜRGERSPITAL WEINSTUBEN
Theaterstrasse 19
Tel: 0931-13861
Sample a local wine, perhaps together with *Weinblatz*, a kind of thick spiced poppadum, or *Weinbeisser* (a long, thin cured sausage).

ZUM STACHEL
Gressengasse 1
Tel: 0931-52770
A venerable establishment dating back to 1413.

Bamberg

RING-VOGEL-HAUS
Pfahlplätzchen 4
Tel: 0951-55080
This wine-cellar is particularly favoured by the locals, as much for its food as for its selection of vintages.

BRUDERMÜHLE
Schranne 1
Tel: 0951-540091
The restaurant has attracted national attention as an excellent place to dine in the region, if not a cheap one.

An Upper Bavarian institution

Bucolic balconies

Pegnitz

PFLAUMS POSTHOTEL PEGNITZ
Nürnbergerstrasse 12-16
Tel: 09241-7250
One of the pre-eminent German restaurants, it serves world-class meals at world-class prices; although the adjacent Posthalterstube has a menu for those on a slightly tighter budget.

Nuremberg

ALBRECHT DÜRER STUBE
Albrecht-Dürer-Strasse 6
Tel: 0911-227209
Just the place to try the delicious *Nürnberger Bratwurst*.

Regensburg

HISTORISCHE WURSTKÜCHE
Adjacent to Stone Bridge (Steinerne Brücke)
Tel: 0941-59098
Tucked into a section of the original city wall, the small kitchen provides food to tourists and locals, either in the smoky interior or at outdoor tables on the bank of the Danube; a visit to Regensburg isn't complete without a stop-off here for a meal or a snack.

ULLI
Watmarkt 4
Tel: 0941-53297
An ideal place to sample the ultra-Bavarian speciality *Dampfnudel* as well as other local specialities.

Try some Saure Lüngerl

Passau

WILDER MANN
Am Rathausplatz
Tel: 0851-35071
One of Passau's oldest and best reputed restaurants on the fifth floor of the hotel.

WEISSER HASE
Ludwigstrasse 23
Tel: 0851-34066
While not enjoying quite the same reputation as Wilder Mann for fine fare, this establishment serves reliable local cuisine at more moderate prices.

Landshut

BEIM VITZTUMB
Landgasse
Tel: 0871-22196
This building's exterior gives a good idea of its cuisine: solid, traditional, and in good taste.

ISAR KLAUSE
Laendstrasse 124 (in summer access from the river)
Tel: 0871-23100
Situated on the Isar this is a good place to sample wine and *Wurst*, or other dishes at affordable prices.

Nightlife

The term 'nightlife' covers a multitude of evils – particularly in Bavaria, where the population is divided between those who want to play all night and those who'd rather just go to bed. Although early closing laws hamper night owls in many areas – this isn't Berlin, where places stay open all night – anyone who wants an evening on the town shouldn't have any problem dancing into the wee hours of the morning in cities like Munich or Würzburg. The large number of concert halls and theatres, meanwhile, makes you remember that Germany was one of the great cradles of Western music; classical music lovers will be in hog heaven.

Dance Fever

Munich discos often close at three or four in the morning; popular venues include the enormous **Park Cafe** (Sophienstrasse 7, Tel: 089-598313), jet-setting **P1** (for the older, richer set, in the Haus der Kunst at Prinzregentenstrasse 1, Tel: 089-294252), and **Nachtwerk** (Landsberger Strasse 185, Tel: 089-9505666), increasingly a venue for good live bands from around the world. In the heart of Schwabing, **Occamstrasse** is lined with a variety of clubs, bars, and

A bar in Munich's Schwabing

Streetlife

discos. Trendy **Nacht Cafe** (Maximilianplatz 5, Tel: 089-595900) is a place to go to hear live music but not necessarily to dance; it's open until 5am (and you can also eat there). By then, **Schmalznudel**, at the Viktualienmarkt, has opened its doors; open only 5am–2pm, this German equivalent of a doughnut shop is the place in Munich to wind down a long night.

In Würzburg, **Sanderstrasse** has a range of pubs (like **Sanders**, Sanderstrasse 7, Tel: 0931-16868); you can also dance at **Café Ludwig**, near the train station (Kaiserstrasse 5, Tel: 0931-51522). Nuremberg's disco **Das Boot** is that city's popular dance venue; people also hang out at the café **Ruhestörung**, or, in summer, on **Albrecht-Dürer-Platz**, carpeted with young people singing, playing guitars, or just talking. In Regensburg, **Skala** is the disco of choice; but fans of ballroom dancing young and old can also go to Tanz Café. Landshut offers, in addition to the disco **Brauhaus** (*see itinerary 15*), the newly renovated **Amadeus** (Isargestade 727, Tel: 0871-22604).

Munich, Augsburg, Würzburg, and Nuremberg, in particular, have become more or less regular stops on the European tours of major pop stars and groups, from Michael Jackson to Metallica. One place to get tickets is at the ticket window in the underground station of Munich's Marienplatz (Tel: 089-229556), where you can also pick up schedules and tickets for other cities.

Another choice for the evening

Garmisch, which has something of a reputation as a playboys' (or rich ski bums') haunt in any case, is one of the few Bavarian towns with a **gambling casino** (Bahnhofstrasse 74, Tel: 08821-53099, daily from 3pm).

Classical Concerts

Of the fifteen itineraries in this book, over half describe places with their own municipal theatres, staging opera and operetta as well as spoken drama (and sometimes exclusively the former) – an indication of just how important old-fashioned art forms like opera are to the man on the street in Europe. In

smaller towns, there won't be a performance every night; your best bet is to check schedules at the tourist information office to see what's on when you get to town.

Opera houses are closed in July and August, but to compensate, there are the summer festivals in Munich and Bayreuth (Munich's **Opernfestspiel** is in July; Bayreuth's Wagner-only **Festspiel** in August). Tickets, alas, are very difficult to come by, especially in Bayreuth, where people spend years on waiting lists before being admitted into the inner sanctum. If all else fails, go to the theatre before the performance and look hopeful; maybe you'll see someone selling a ticket (*Karte*). It's easier to gain access to the open-air summer performances at the amphitheatre by the **Roter Tor** in Augsburg.

The state of orchestral music in Germany is equally healthy: Munich alone has four major orchestras. The Munich Philharmonic plays in the magnificent *Philharmoniesaal*, one of a number of evening venues situated in the modern Gasteig Culture Centre.

Apart from Munich and Bayreuth, Bamberg has placed itself solidly on the international music map with its world-class orchestra; and literally every one of these Bavarian cities has a concert schedule any town should be proud of. Again, this doesn't end in summer, which sees various festivals such as Würzburg's **Mozart Festival** in June, featuring great musicians playing in the gardens of the Residence. Garmisch, in July, celebrates the work of local boy Richard Strauss.

Other Pursuits

Of course, in Bavaria there are legion other things to do at night, from spending an evening in one of Rothenburg's puppet shows at **Am Burgtor** to attending a cabaret performance in Munich's traditional **Drehleier** (Balanstrasse 23, Tel: 089-484337) or the **Lustspielhaus** on Occamstrasse, where you sit at tables with little lamps on them, 1920s-style, to drinking late into the night at a beer hall or village *Volksfest*.

The **Kinocenter Garmisch and Aspentheater im Lamm** (Marienplatz, Tel: 08821-2470) in Garmisch-Partenkirchen is a pleasant cinema which screens current English-language films; both Munich's **Cinema** (Nymphenburger Strasse 31, Tel: 089-555255) and **Museum Lichtspiele** (Ludwigsbrücke, Tel: 089-482403) also include many English-language films on their extensive programmes. All three sell popcorn.

Calendar of Special Events

Between Catholic holidays and local traditions, Bavaria is without doubt the festival capital of Germany. Its towns host such a wide variety of folk festivals and traditional fairs that there is something going on somewhere almost any time of year.

FEBRUARY/MARCH

11 November, at 11.11am, is the official beginning of Germany's Carnival season, but the real celebrating doesn't start until a few weeks before **Faschingsdienstag** (Shrove Tuesday, or Mardi Gras). On the Tuesday itself, Bavaria takes half a day off, and towns fill with crowds of costumed revellers anxious to squeeze in a last bit of excess before the rigours of Lent close in. For this fasting season, Bavarian monks brewed their beer extra-strong to compensate for the pangs of hunger. Hence Munich's **Strong Beer Festival** (*Starkbierfest*) in early March at the Salvatorkeller am Nockherberg, where people get down to some serious drinking.

Knights at Kaltenberg

MAY/JUNE

The Thursday after Trinity Sunday, which usually falls in early June, is **Fronleichnam**, Corpus Christi. Streets are lined with green tree branches, and processions of priests and singers bear banners and holy images through town. Near Füssen, on the lake Forggensee, the procession is borne across the water on boats.

Every fourth year, at the end of June, the city of Landshut celebrates its Wedding. Not just any wedding, but the marriage of George, Duke Ludwig the Rich's eldest son, which took place in 1475. Regarded as impressively excessive at the time, the Wedding is re-enacted in the course of a three-week folk festival. The next **Landshuter Hochzeit** will be held from 26 June to 18 July 1993.

Held every tenth year from May to September is the **Passion Play** at Oberammergau, a day-long performance re-enacting the life of Christ. The next performance is scheduled for the year 2000.

At the Oktoberfest

JULY/AUGUST

Bavarian villages herald the lazy days of summer with special festivals of their own. In Franconia, nearly every weekend sees a **wine festival** (*Weinfest*) in a different town. A major Franconian folk festival is the **Kiliani** in Würzburg, held the first two weeks of July.

In Lower Bavaria, beer is drunk at village folk festivals; one such fair is Straubing's popular *Gäubodenfest* in August. The Upper Bavarian town of Mittenwald returns to its roots with a **Renaissance Folk Festival** in the last two weeks of July. Equally old-fashioned, but more energetic, is the **Kaltenberger Ritterturnier**, a medieval tournament in a village just north of Ammersee, also held in July.

On the Romantic Road, Dinkels-bühl has a special July festival, too. In 1632, so it's said, children saved the town by running out in front of the Swedish army and begging for mercy. Today, the **Dinkelsbühler Kinderzeche** is commemorated with a cheerful ten-day festival, around the third Monday in July.

SEPTEMBER/OCTOBER

Every autumn, the cows which have grazed all summer in the Alps are adorned with flowers and driven back through the village streets to their barns for the winter. This custom, the **Albabtrieb**, is an excuse for much festivity in Upper Bavarian towns, particularly Garmisch, in late September or early October.

September also sees the beginning of Munich's **Oktoberfest**, which runs for two weeks and three weekends, ending the first weekend in October. The Theresienwiese, the site on which the event is held, is converted into a small city visited by some 8 million people. But the fairground is a sideshow to the main purpose of the festivities, namely the consumption of beer which takes place in massive tents set up by the city's six brewers.

NOVEMBER

St Leonard's Day falls on 6 November. The patron saint of animals is honoured by farmers who hang his picture on stable doors and along Alpine paths. The custom of having one's horses blessed and then riding around the town church, **Leonardiritt**, has developed into a festival in Bad Tölz, Benediktbeuren and other Upper Bavarian towns.

DECEMBER

In early December little wooden huts spring up in the main squares of cities and towns, selling Christmas ornaments, local crafts, and hot mulled wine (*Glühwein*). Most famous of these **Christmas markets** is the original one in Nuremberg, renowned for its gingerbread (*Lebkuchen*).

On 6 December, you may run into St Nicholas himself, distributing gifts to the children, accompanied by *Krampus*, who carries soot for naughty boys and girls.

As his day falls on 31 December, St **Sylvester** has given his name to the German New Year's Eve, celebrated everywhere with plenty of fireworks and plenty of champagne.

GETTING THERE

By Air

Opened in May 1992, the new Munich airport offers services to most worldwide destinations. When you arrive, follow signs to the green S for S-Bahn, the train to the city centre. The journey takes about half an hour, about the same time as a taxi; but bear in mind that a taxi can cost around DM100.

TRAVEL ESSENTIALS

When to Visit

If I were planning a trip to Bavaria, I'd go in May, August to October, or December. In May, you risk spring showers – but you always risk showers when you travel in Central Europe, and you're rewarded with the sight of blossoming apple trees and forsythia on the green hills. Late summer, the one time when the region can be pretty much counted on to be warm, means lounging in country beer gardens, boating on the lakes or hiking in the mountains. September puts a nip in the air and turns everything in the country gold, with a blue-and-white sky the colours of the diamonds on the Bavarian flag. And while the weather in December may be cold, snow brings ski season; while the illuminated wooden stalls

Munich airport

of *Christkindl* markets transform cities and towns into picture-postcard holiday fantasies.

Weather

The only thing you can be sure of about Bavarian weather – indeed, about Central European weather in general – is that it may well rain, especially in any month that isn't July or August. You can also expect it to be grey, and sometimes fiercely cold, in winter. Not to say that there aren't many warm, sunny days between April and October; and summers seem to be getting increasingly hot.

Despite its lakes, Bavaria is a landlocked region, and anyone coming from a humid climate will notice how dry it is. Another peculiarity is the wind called *Föhn*. A result of climatic conditions created by the mountains, the wind, which

causes headaches and mood swings (in fact, the *Föhn* defence will stand up in court), is likely to be blowing on sunny, crystal-clear days, when the mountains seem close enough to touch. It's particularly noticeable if you're in a car; drivers seem to go crazy on *Föhn* days.

The altitude also makes people very sensitive to their circulatory systems; *Kreislaufstörungen* (circulatory disorders) are a common ailment. The traditional treatment is a glass of champagne; the bubbles, it seems, are very good indeed for your circulation.

Clothing

Whatever the season, make sure you pack a few warm clothes, a sweater or jacket, and, in winter, a warm coat. If you're arriving in summer, however, you'll need some real hot-weather garb – and don't forget to bring a bathing suit in case you want to dip into a mountain lake or one of the clean, park-like public pools. Good walking shoes are vital.

Electricity

Bavarian outlets have standard European voltage: 220v. If you're coming from the UK, you'll need a plug adaptor before your appliance will work with a German socket; Americans need AC adaptors, as well, to convert the voltage.

Time Differences

All of Germany is in the same, Central European time zone, which means that it's one hour later in Germany than it is in Great Britain, six hours later than it is in Boston, and nine hours later than Seattle.

GETTING ACQUAINTED

Geography

Bavaria is the southernmost state of Germany, bordering on Austria to the south and the Czech Republic to the east. Its entire southern border is drawn along the Alps; another mountainous region is the range running through the Bavarian Forest, the Upper Palatinate Forest, and the Fichtel Mountains, bordering on the Czech Republic.

Traditionally, Bavaria's northern border was formed by the River Danube (*Donau*); today, the state extends much farther north. The Danube is only one of several major rivers that have formed trade routes from time immemorial, including the Isar, Inn, and Lech flowing up into it from the south, and the Main in Franconia (a canal linking the Main with the Danube was opened in late 1992, completing a route of waterways reaching from the North Sea to the Black Sea). Bavaria – particularly Upper Bavaria – is also famous for its many beautiful lakes.

Government and Economy

The Free State of Bavaria is the largest of the 16 German states, and is, like them, represented in both the Parliament and the Senate (*Bundestag* and *Bundesrat*) of the Federal Government. It is, however, the only German state to have its own *Senat* as well as the usual State Parliament (*Landtag*). Below these in authority are the governments of the seven provinces which comprise the state.

Since the war, Bavaria has traditionally been arch-conservative, with its own majority political party, the CSU, which is even farther right than the conservative party of the rest of Germany, the CDU. The CSU was led for years by Franz-Josef Strauss, whose 'reign' ended with his death in 1988; since then, his party has lost quite a bit of its popular support. One of Bavaria's ironies is that this conservative bastion is governed from the city of Munich, where the party in power is the left-wing SPD, in a coalition with the Green Party.

Traditionally agricultural, and still Germany's leading food producer, Bavaria has become increasingly important as a centre for science and big business since the war. Although the farmhouses and grazing cattle aren't likely to vanish from the landscape, they've had to make room for edifices like the huge BMW plant in Dingolfing. Siemens, it's said, has employed one out of every ten Bavarians at some point in its history. And, with the arrival of computer companies from home and abroad on the scene, the area around Munich is unofficially known as 'Germany's Silicon Valley'. Munich is a favourite site for trade fairs and expositions, making it a focal point for industries from fashion, watches and jewellery to computers and cars.

Religion

Asked to describe his countrymen in an English-language assignment for school, a child I know wrote, 'The Bavarians are short and dark, and they are Catholic'. Whether or not it's because of the heritage of the *Baiuvarii* tribe which settled here after the Romans left, it's true that Bavarians tend to have the dark complexions of natives of southern climes.

As far as religion is concerned, although Protestantism came into some parts of Franconia in the 16th century, the region continues to be predominantly Catholic − a fact most noticeable from the many public and bank holidays, such as Corpus Christi or Assumption Day, which can come as a complete surprise to Protestant visitors (or absent-minded residents, for that matter). Catholicism is also evident in the common salutation *Grüß Gott*, God's greeting, which replaces *Guten Tag* (good day) in this part of the German-speaking world (don't use it, however, in Frankfurt or Hamburg, unless you want to be the object of much merriment).

Currency

The basic unit of German currency is a mark (DM), divided into 100 pfennigs. Coins come in 1, 2, 5, 10, and 50 pfennig denominations, as well as 1, 2, and 5 marks; notes start at 10 and go up. New currency was introduced in the late 1980s, which means that you may have two different kinds of DM20 notes to deal with; the new ones are very flashy, with lots of extra features such as a silver strip running through the note or the numbers in Braille under the printed number.

Credit cards are not widely used (and American Express is not very popular; retailers much prefer other cards). If you haven't got Eurocheques, you'll often have to pay *bar* (cash). Nearly every town has an automatic teller which accepts Eurocards, as well, sometimes, as other credit cards. In Munich, near Marienplatz, the Sparkasse has automatic tellers which exchange foreign bills for German currency. If you're not near such a facility, you'll have to find a *Wechselstube* (currency exchange). In large cities, the railway station often has a bank which is open later than 3.30pm; in Munich, it's open until 10pm.

Tipping

As a service charge is included in restaurant prices, it's customary to show appreciation for good service simply by rounding up the bill a mark or two when you pay the waitress. The same rule holds true in taxis. In big hotels, however, international tipping customs still hold.

By Train

German trains are fast, efficient, and expensive. If you're 26 or under, you qualify for youth fares; while if travelling a long distance over a weekend, you may qualify for a special saver's fare (*Sparpreis* or *Supersparpreis*, depending on the distance), a round-trip discount which allows a second person to come along for half price. For short distances, however, there's very little you can do except grin

and pay up. To compensate for this, you'll find there are several connections a day to virtually anywhere you want to go.

Special train lines are added vacation attractions in certain areas, such as the funicular train from Garmisch up the Zugspitze; the steam locomotive that runs through Franconia's 'Little Switzerland'; or the little locomotive that carries passengers to and from the ferry dock at Chiemsee.

BAYERISCHE ZUGSPITZBAHN
Olympiastrasse 27, Garmisch
Tel: 08821-7970
Responsible for funicular trains and cable cars up the Zugspitze. English brochure available.

FRANCONIAN SWITZERLAND STEAM TRAIN
(Dampfbahn Fränkische Schweiz)
Postfach 1, 8553 Ebermannstadt
Tel: 09131-65873
Sunday service between Forchheim/ Beringersmühle and Ebermannstadt on vintage trains from the 1930s, May– September.

CHIEMSEE-BAHN
Seestrasse 108, Prien
Tel: 08051-6090
105-year-old rail service from Prien to the ferry dock at Stock (2km).

Bus, Tram, Underground

German public transport works on an honours system, which often seems more complicated than need be. Tickets are available from vendors sporting a 'K' over their kiosks, or from automats in underground stations and even on trams. After you buy a ticket, you have to cancel it in a small machine marked with an

'E'. Conductors check periodically to make sure everyone is legal; fines are annoyingly steep if you're caught. Most cities offer day tickets which allow unlimited travel after morning rush hour, or family tickets allowing several people to go together.

By Car

Introduced in the 1930s, the German *Autobahn* has achieved something of a legendary status in Europe. If you've always dreamed of being in a Formula One race, you could really enjoy the *Autobahn* experience. There are no speed limits, and you can count on being passed by a streamlined BMW no matter how fast you're going. If you want to see the countryside at leisure, however, it's best to take the regular *Bundesstrassen* (B).

One way of getting around

Business Hours

In Germany, business hours are strictly controlled. Shops are generally open from 8 or 9am to 6pm; in smaller towns or less central neighbourhoods, they often close for lunch. On Saturdays, they close at 1 or 2pm, except for the first Saturday of the month, *langer Samstag*, when stores in town centres are open until 4pm. Recently instituted, amid much discussion, is 'long Thursday', *langer Donnerstag*, when many establishments stay open until 8 or 9pm, and even banks, which normally close at 3.30pm, are open until 5.30pm. On Sundays, all you'll find open are bakeries which double as cafés and shops at the railway stations or airports which charge exorbitant prices.

Public Holidays

Bavaria has so many public holidays it's hard to keep track of them. A partial listing:

New Year's Day
Epiphany (*Heilige Drei Könige*)
Shrove Tuesday (*Faschingsdienstag*)
  (shops close at noon)
Good Friday (*Karfreitag*)
Easter Monday
Ascension Day (*Christi Himmelfahrt*)
Whit Monday (*Pfingstmontag*)
Corpus Christi (*Fronleichnam*)
Assumption Day (*Maria Himmelfahrt*)
German Unity Day 3 October
Day of Repentance and Prayer (*Buss- und Bettag*) 18 November
Christmas Eve (*Heiliger Abend*)
First and Second Christmas Days (*1. und 2. Weihnachtstag*)

ACCOMMODATION

In the summer months, it can be very difficult to find a hotel room in the Alpine regions of Bavaria. Virtually every farmhouse, however, offers rooms for rent (*Zimmer, Fremdenzimmer*), and often these accommodations are as pleasant and comfortable as any you'll find – and cheaper than some.

In the listing below, approximate prices for a double room are given as *$* = DM70–100; *$$* = DM150–200; *$$$* = DM200+.

Munich

The season you should avoid, or book months in advance, is Oktoberfest in Munich (the last two weeks in September, through early October). There's not a hotel bed to be had. All the international hotel chains are represented in Munich. Here is a small selection of more intimate establishments, recommended for their comfort and convenience.

HOTEL LEOPOLD
Leopoldstrasse 119, Munich 40
Tel: 089-367061
Located in northern Schwabing, a five-minute walk from Münchner Freiheit, this small hotel, although on busy

Flower arrangements in Rothenburg

Leopoldstrasse, is comfortable, conveniently located, and has an in-house restaurant. *$$*

HOTEL HABIS
Maria Theresia Strasse 2a, Munich 80
Tel: 089-4705071
Located in Haidhausen just to the east of the river Isar in front of the park behind the Bavarian Parliament building. Excellent restaurant with live piano on Fridays and Saturdays. *$$*

PENSION FRANK
Schellingstrasse 24, Munich 40
Tel: 089-281451
In the heart of Schwabing, this pension is renowned as the place where models stay when in Munich for photo shoots. *$/$$*

HOTEL KÖNIGSWACHE
Steinheilstrasse 7, Munich 2
Tel: 089-522001
A clean, mid-priced hotel located a short walk from the museums, near the Technical University, with a Chinese restaurant on the ground floor. *$$*

The Alps (Upper Bavaria)

Füssen and Environs

ZUM HECHTEN
Ritterstrasse 6, 8958 Füssen
Tel: 08362-7906 or 6801
In the old city centre, not far from the river, a pleasant establishment complete with restaurant. *$*

A typical Gaststätte in Upper Bavaria

HOTEL ALPENSCHLÖSSLE
Alatseestrasse 28, 8958 Füssen (Bad Faulenbach)
Tel: 08362-4017
Pleasant surroundings and fine dining. *$$*

Garmisch/Grainau

EIBSEE HOTEL
8104 Grainau-Eibsee
Tel: 08821-8081
A luxurious hotel with a wonderful view. If you're up for an Alpine splurge, this is the place. *$$$*

Mittenwald

HOTEL ALPENROSE
Obermarkt 1, 8102 Mittenwald
Tel: 08823-5055
An old Bavarian establishment at the heart of town. *$/$$*

POST-HOTEL
Obermarkt 9, 8102 Mittenwald
Tel: 08823-1094
Also central, but outfitted with more luxurious trappings such as sauna, solarium, etc. *$$*

Berchtesgaden and Environs

ALPENHOTEL KRONPRINZ
Kälbersteinstrasse 8
8240 Berchtesgaden
Tel: 08652-6070
A short walk from the centre, near the railway station, this comfortable hotel offers luxuries (sauna etc), a restaurant (dinner only), and a mountain view. *$$*

HOTEL-GASTHOF NUTZKASER
Am Gseng 10, 8243 Ramsau
Tel: 08657-388 or 619
A country hotel with panoramic view and good, cheap restaurant. *$*

Romantic Road

Augsburg

HOTEL ULRICH
Kapuzinergasse 6, 8900 Augsburg
Tel: 0821-33077
Just off of Maximilianstr., this hotel is near enough to be within an easy walk of sights and nightlife, but located on a quiet narrow street. *$$*

Dinkelsbühl

WEISSES ROSS
Steingasse 12, 8804 Dinkelsbühl
Tel: 09851-2274
A renovated stable, with rooms furnished in a modern Bavarian style, forms the second of this hotel's two buildings. *$/$$*

Rothenburg

BURG HOTEL
Klostergasse 1–3, 8803 Rothenburg ob der Tauber
Tel: 09861-5037
You can't beat the romance of this ivy-covered hotel with individually-furnished rooms and suites, each with a view out over the Tauber valley. *$$$*

Würzburg

HOTEL REBSTOCK
Neubaustrasse 7, 8700 Würzburg
Tel: 0931-30930
Elegant, glossy, and in the heart of downtown, with a renowned restaurant. *$$$*

GASTHOF GOLDENER HAHN
Marktgasse 7, 8700 Würzburg
Tel: 0931-51941
Modest yet centrally located, with single rooms starting at DM35. *$/$$*

Franconia

Bamberg

BRUDERMÜHLE
Schranne 1, 8600 Bamberg
Tel: 0951-54091
A pleasant hotel at the heart of the old city. *$$*

ST NEPOMUK UND GÄSTEHÄUSER
Obere Mühlbrücke 9, 8600 Bamberg
Tel: 0951-25183
Right on the river. *$$*

Bayreuth

ZUR LOHMÜHLE
Badstrasse 7, 8580 Bayreuth
Tel: 0921-53060
Nice little hotel with restaurant, both
bordering on the stream powering the
mill for which the place is named. *$$*

Pegnitz

PFLAUMS POSTHOTEL PEGNITZ
Nürnbergerstrasse 12–16, 8570 Pegnitz
Tel: 09241-7250
The preferred accommodation for
Bayreuth Festival-goers. *$$$*

Nuremberg

HOTEL FACKELMANN
Essenweinstrasse 10, 8500 Nürnberg
Tel: 0911-204121
A short walk from the city centre, near
the railway station, in a modern part of
the city. *$$*

HAUS AM SCHÖNEN BRUNNEN
Hauptmarkt, 8500 Nürnberg
Tel: 0911-224225
Right on the main square. Reserve in ad-
vance for *Christkindlmarkt. $$*

Niederbayern/Lower Bavaria

Passau

HOTEL WILDER MANN
Am Rathausplatz, 8390 Passau
Tel: 0851-35071
One of Passau's oldest hotels, containing
the Glass Museum. *$$*

HOTEL ZUM KÖNIG
Rindermarkt 2, 8390 Passau
Tel: 0851-34098

Sign of hospitality

The yellow-and-white baroque facade
alone is worth the price of a room –
which is surprisingly low. *$/$$*

Regensburg and Environs

BISCHOFSHOF
Kräuterermarkt 3, 8400 Regensburg
Tel: 0941-59086
Just behind the Cathedral, this comfortable yet affordable hotel has a number of
different (and reputable) restaurants offering everything from fine dining (try
the Danube fish) to rustic Bavarian charm
– as well as an in-house brand of beer. *$$*

HOTEL KRIEGER
8411 Mariaort, 8400 Regensburg
Tel: 0941-80018
In a lovely location on the banks of the
Naab river, 10km (6 miles) from Regens-
burg, with plenty of countryside walks,
this is a family-run hotel with a distinctly
Bavarian flavour. *$*

Landshut

HOTEL GOLDENE SONNE
Neustadt 520, 8300 Landshut
Tel: 0871-23087
An old-timey *Gasthof* in operation since
1400, complete with restaurant and its
own beer garden. *$$*

COMMUNICATIONS & MEDIA

Dialling internationally is straightfor-
ward. The international code from Germany is 00. After this, dial the country
code: Australia (61); Italy (39); Japan
(81); the Netherlands (31); Spain (34);
United Kingdom (44); United States and
Canada (1). Long-distance calls can be
made from the Post Office, which saves
you having to pay the higher charges
levied by hotels. If using a US phone
credit card, dial the company's access
number: AT&T, Tel: 0130-0010; MCI,
Tel: 0130-0012; Sprint, Tel: 0130-0013.

The early evening news

The American Armed Forces Network broadcasting from Nuremberg went off the air in December 1992. Voice of America and Radio Free Europe are both still transmitting English-language programmes, and an Austrian station called Blue Danube Radio features programmes of oldies and big-band music.

In Munich, the English-language magazine *Munich Found*, available at many kiosks and at the train stations, contains information about the city and surrounding area, as well as a variety of interesting articles and activity suggestions.

USEFUL INFORMATION

Disabled Facilities

The well-organised system of tourist information offices (*Fremdenverkehrsämter*) throughout Bavaria makes it fairly easy to get information about handicapped facilities in the various cities. Augsburg, for example, has prepared an entire brochure entiled *Leben in der Gemeinschaft* (Living in the Community), filled with useful addresses and phone numbers of everything from doctors to hotels to public phones which are accessible by wheelchair.

While wheelchair users will have difficulty using city buses and trams, the underground in Munich has been installing more and more lifts in recent years, making virtually every stop accessible to the handicapped. Public buildings erected in recent years, such as the Gasteig Culture Centre, also tend to be fully equipped with toilets and phones for the handicapped; older buildings, such as museums and libraries, are being fitted out with access ramps and lifts.

For Children

Bavaria is filled with wonderful things to do with children, from boat excursions on the Danube to a visit to the Bavaria Film Studio in Munich (089-64990), which offers the German version of Hollywood studio tour. Rothenburg ob der Tauber and Nuremberg both have Doll and Toy Museums (in Rothenburg at Hofbronnengasse 13. Tel: 09681/7330; in Nuremberg at Karlstr. 13–15, Tel: 0911-2313164). In Dinkelsbühl, the small

Museum of the Third Dimension presents simple, hands-on exhibits of optical illusions, stereoscopic slides, and the like (Nördlinger Tor/Stadtmühle, Tel: 09851-6336). To visit Munich's Deutsches Museum (address see *Museums*) can take days: but the coal mine is a hit amongst the children. The same goes for the salt mine in Berchtesgaden.

If you're looking for performances suitable for children, Germany is the right place to be: the major orchestras often give children's concerts, which generally involve some explanation and some audience participation as well as a child-oriented musical or theatre programme. It has been my experience that even children with no German at all enjoy these a great deal. One ambitious Munich Philharmonic soloist arranged a performance of Prokofiev's *Peter and the Wolf* for which the entire audience of children were provided with kazoos; the result was a kind of international communication that left everyone over the age of 12 with a major headache. A full listing of all such concerts in English can be found in the calendar section of Munich's monthly English-language magazine, *Munich Found*.

Museums

Munich

Alte Pinakothek
One of the great European collections of Old Masters, including room after room of masterpieces by Peter Paul Rubens.

Neue Pinakothek
Situated next to the Alte Pinakothek, this museum concentrates on 19th-century European painting.

Lenbachhaus
Built as a residence by the painter Franz Lenbach, the pretty yellow villa contains the seminal collection of works by the Expressionist *Blaue Reiter* school (including Kandinsky, Klee, and Marc), and also presents modern exhibitions.

Münchner Stadtmuseum
City history, from the wooden Moorish dancers to the photography museum, as well as a wide variety of rotating exhibitions, and a film museum with classic English-language films.

Deutsches Museum
The world's largest museum of science and technology with hands-on exhibits about everything from coal mining to astronomy. The 'Forum of Technology' contains Germany's first IMAX cinema.

Glyptothek
Displays of ancient Greek and Roman sculpture.

Jagdmuseum
On the pedestrian precinct near Karlsplatz. A display of all manner of trophies demonstrates the Bavarian passion for hunting.

BMW Museum
In a futuristic building near the Olympic Park. A fascinating look at the development of the ultimate driving machine.

Füssen
Museum of the City of Füssen
Exhibitions on the city's history include a description of the craft of lute-making.

Garmisch
Freilichtmuseum an der Glenleiten
Amerang (Kochel/Murnau exit from A95/Garmisch Autobahn). Open year round. This is the largest open-air museum in Bavaria and consists of a selection of authentic buildings moved here

from the different regions, designed to show traditional rural lifestyles and architecture. Among the main attractions are a watermill and a blacksmith's.

Mittenwald
Museum of Violin-Making
Instruments and documents pertaining to the town's traditional craft.

Berchtesgaden
Schloss Museum
From wooden sculptures to city history to the furnished rooms of the Wittelsbach's summer palace, it's all here in the Romanesque or baroque rooms of this rambling palace.

Augsburg
Staatsgalerie in the Schaezler Palace
Wonderful painting collection in a baroque residential palace. Don't feel obliged, though, to see the adjacent Baroque Gallery.

Roman Museum
Relics from the first heyday of this former Roman capital, located in an old Dominican church.

Swabian Crafts Museum (*Handwerker Museum*)
Traditional local crafts, complementing the *Handwerker Route* through the city where you can see craftsmen still practising their trades.

Rothenburg
Museum of Crime
From stocks to the infamous Iron Maiden, a comprehensive history of medieval punishment. Exhibits explained in English.

Imperial City Museum
Located in a restored 13th-century Dominican monastery, exhibits about the city's history from the Stone Age to the present (including life in the monastery).

Inside the Glenleiten museum

Würzburg

Mainfränkisches Museum
Located in the baroque *Zeughaus* on Marienburg, this museum has a fantastic collection of Franconian art and cultural objects.

Bamberg

Diocesan Museum
Treasures from the religious history of the city, from Byzantine fabrics and hangings to baroque.

History Museum
Cultural and art history of the region around Bamberg.

Franconian Brewing Museum
Items historically used for beer production, suitably displayed in an old monastery brewery.

Karl May Museum
The home of the popular author whose books have been loved by generations of young Germans.

Bayreuth

Haus Wahnfried
Richard Wagner's home is a museum dedicated to him, complete with scores and other memorabilia.

Tüchersfeld

Franconian Switzerland Museum (*Fränkische Schweiz Museum*)
Exhibits about geology, regional living, and Jewish culture, located in an 18th-century complex of Jewish buildings.

Nuremberg

Germanisches Nationalmuseum
Founded in the 19th century, this is a museum for all of Germany with painting and sculpture, toys and textiles, and German history from prehistoric times to the present.

Transport Museum (*Verkehrsmuseum*)
A look at the history of transport, in the city that saw the first German railroad in 1835.

Zwiesel

Forest Museum (*Waldmuseum Zwiesel*)
Exhibits about the Bavarian Forest, Zwiesel glass and local traditions and lifestyles.

Glass Museum
Glass creations old and new.

Tittling/Bavarian Forest

Farmer's Museum (open-air)
One of the best of Bavaria's open-air museums, where various old farm buildings and dwellings have been moved from all over the region to give a flavour of daily life in the past.

Classical forms in Munich's Glyptothek

Passau

Museum in the Veste Oberhaus
In the hilltop castle, Passau cultural history and an observation tower.

Roman Museum/Boiotro Castle
Prehistory and archeology, as well as excavations of Roman ruins.

Passau Glass Museum
Over 30,000 glasses document 200 years of glass-making history. Located in the hotel Wilder Mann.

Regensburg

Castle Museum (*Schlossmuseum*)
Former monastery building redone in the 19th century as the sumptuous palace of the Counts of Thurn und Taxis.

Diocesan Museum St Ulrich
Gothic art treasures displayed in an old church building.

Museum of the City of Regensburg
History, art and culture of Eastern Bavaria.

Landshut

City Museum and City Painting Collection in the Residence
In the former, artifacts from prehistoric times, the Romans, and the Middle Ages; in the latter, German painters from the 16th–19th centuries.

LANGUAGE

Hard to speak and even harder to understand, the Bavarian dialect involves a lot of rounded, long vowels and swallowed word endings. In general, negotiations in halting High German (*Hochdeutsch*) are preferable to attempts to master the local argot – unless you've lived in Bavaria for quite a while. But some elements of the following mini-glossary – such as greetings and leave-takings – are 100 percent Bavarian.

Note that the letter which looks like a funny B (ß) is actually a double S (Straße is the same as Strasse). Umlauts over vowels – ä, ö, ü – are the equivalent of placing an E after the vowel (*schön*, beautiful, is the same as *schoen*), and pronounced by pursing your lips as you speak the word. Often, this simply has the effect of Americanising the purer, European vowels – at McDonald's, a favourite meal is the 'Big Mäc'. Nouns, by the way, are always written with capital letters. In some cases, phonetic approximations are given of the terms below.

Greetings and Numbers

Greeting	*Grüß Gott*
Goodbye	*Tschüß*; *Ade*; *Servus* (as well as *Auf Wiedersehen*, high German)
Please	*Bitte* (or *bitte schön*)
Thank you	*Danke* (or *danke schön*)
How much?	*Wieviel* (vee feel)
What time...	*Wieviel Uhr*
Where is...	*Wo ist...*
Left, right	*Links*, *rechts*
Straight on	*Geradeaus*
City map	*Stadtplan*
Do you have...	*Haben Sie...*
I need...	*Ich brauche...*
I'd like...	*Ich möchte...*
Pay	*Bezahlen*
(also used to request the bill at a restaurant: *Bezahlen*, *bitte*)	
Receipt	*Quittung*
Single room	*Einzelzimmer*
Double room	*Doppelzimmer*
One night	*Eine Nacht*
Two nights	*zwei Nächte*
Shower	*Dusche* (doo-sha)
Bathroom	*Toilette* (twa-letta), *Klo*, *WC* (vey sey)

Women	*Damen* (dahmen)
Men	*Herren* (hairen)
Children	*Kinder*
Shop	*Geschäft*, *Laden*
Clothes	*Kleider*
one	*eins*
two	*zwei*
three	*drei*
four	*vier*
five	*fünf*
six	*sechs*
seven	*sieben*
eight	*acht*
nine	*neun*
ten	*zehn*
twenty	*zwanzig*

Food

This listing of Bavarian and German words may help you determine what to look for on the average menu.

Semmel	roll
Brez'n	pretzel
Knödel	dumpling
Spätzle	small, chewy noodles
Kartoffel	potato
Kraut, *Kohl*	cabbage
Rosenkohl	Brussels sprouts
Pepperoni	hot green peppers
Zwiebel	onion
Knoblauch	garlic
Schweinsbraten	roast pork
Rinderbraten	roast beef
Kalb	veal
Kalbskopf	calf's head
Ochsenschwanz	oxtail
Hax'n	pork knuckle
Rippchen	ribs
Lüngeri	lungs
Nieren	kidneys
Leber	liver
Zunge	tongue
Schinken	ham
Pute, *Truthahn*	turkey
Geschnetzeltes	meat in small pieces
Schnitzel	cutlet
Gulasch	meat stew
Spiegelei	fried egg
Helles	light (beer)
Dunkles	dark (beer)
Spezi	Coke and orange soda mix
Apfelschorle	half apple juice, half mineral water

Hiking

If you like to walk, Bavaria is a good place to visit. Nearly every region has a network of well-marked trails, and tourist offices are happy to hand out free maps of interesting routes. In the Alps, you can often take a cable car ride to the top of a peak, then enjoy the beautiful walk back down. From many of the summits hanggliders and paragliders take the quick way into the valley.

The mountains are also filled with Alpine huts (*Hütten*) where walkers can stay the night (in rough-and-ready surroundings), enabling you to go on jaunts of several days. Further information is available from the **Deutsche Alpenverein** (Praterinsel 5, 8000 München 22, Tel: 089-2350900).

Franconian Switzerland is just one region with a programme called 'Hiking without Luggage' (*Wandern ohne Gepäck*), five- to seven-day walking routes where your luggage is taken from inn to inn, and is waiting for you at your destination at the end of the day (for information, contact the Franconian Switzerland Tourist Office, address below).

Cycling

Bicycles can be rented in most towns, sometimes from the German Railroad (*Deutsche Bundesbahn*) or from private shops. In Garmisch, **Ferdi's Werkstatt** (Promenadestrasse 14) rents mountain bikes to anyone ready to tackle the Alps; but it's the more level trails along the rivers that draw cyclists in real numbers. The Danube, the Isar, and the Inn are all lined with cycle paths (*Radwege*) on which you can make trips of several days (cycling, if you've a mind to, all the way to Vienna or even Hungary), alternating with travel on certain designated trains where you can take your bike free of charge. Again, tourist offices are well-stocked with maps and plenty of information: notably Passau (the Danube and Inn routes) and Landshut (the Isar route).

Boating

Lakes Starnberg, Tegernsee, Ammersee, and Chiemsee are just a few of the larger Bavarian lakes that offer boating (not to mention the small ones throughout the Alps). To rent a boat on Chiemsee, whether you want a sailboat (*Segelboot*), rowboat (*Ruderboot*), or paddle-boat (*Tretboot*), call **Bootsverleih G Schraml** (Harrasser Strasse, Tel: 08051-4575) or **Bootsverleih Schwarz** (Seestrasse, Tel: 08051-61063). Bavaria's rivers also offer plenty of boating opportunities. In Franconian Switzerland, the adventurous can rent a kayak from **Schottersmühle** (8551 Waischenfeld, Tel: 09196-1503; near Beringersmühle) and set off down the river Wiesent. If you'd prefer something bigger, try an excursion along the Danube from Passau or Regensburg (one major line is **Donauschiffahrt Wurm & Köck**, Tel: 0851-929292). The various cruise

A popular means of descent

A skier's paradise

companies offer trips ranging from afternoon jaunts along the Danube (taking in such sights as the canyon called Donaudurchbruch) to longer outings to cities as far away as Vienna. Enquire at the East Bavarian Tourist Office about passenger trips along the new Rhine-Main-Danube Canal (see *p 104*).

Skiing

In Upper Bavaria, you're in the heart of ski country. Garmisch is a special ski centre (68 miles of downhill trails, 93 of cross-country), but the mountains are criss-crossed with networks of chair lifts, cable cars, and ski trails of all descriptions. Detailed information about trails, package offers, and the like are readily available from the tourist information centres (especially Garmisch, Mittenwald, Berchtesgaden). There are also legion ski schools, for both cross-country and downhill. Special attraction in Garmisch is the Zugspitzplatt, Germany's only skiable glacier.

Remember, though, that the Alps don't have the only skiing in Bavaria. The Bavarian Forest is full of slopes (again, both downhill and cross-country); Zwiesel, for example, has an active winter season with ski schools and rental facilities, and has even hosted World Cup races.

USEFUL ADDRESSES

German Tourist Offices Abroad

Australia
German National Tourist Office, Lufthansa House, 9th Floor, 143 Macquarie Street, Sydney 2000. Tel: (012) 367 38 90, Fax: (012) 367 38 95

Austria
Deutsche Zentrale für Tourismus (DZT), Schubertring 12, A-1010 Wien. Tel: (22) 513 27 92, Fax: (22) 513 27 91

Canada
German National Tourist Office, 175 Bloor Street East, North Tower, Suite 604, Toronto, Ontario, M4W 3R8. Tel: (416) 968 15 70, Fax: (416) 968 19 86

Denmark
Tysk Turist-Information, Vesterbrogade 6 D III, DK-1620 Copenhagen V. Tel: (33) 12 70 95, Fax: (33) 14 47 47

France
Office National Allemand du Tourisme, 9 Boulevard de la Madeleine, F-75001 Paris. Tel: (31) 40 20 01 88, Fax: (31) 42 86 02 17

Hong Kong
German National Tourist Office, c/o Lufthansa German Airlines, Landmark East, 5th Floor, 12 Ice House Street, Hong Kong. Tel: (052) 846 63 88, Fax: (052) 810 06 01

Israel
German National Tourist Office, c/o Lufthansa German Airlines, 1 Ben-Yehuda Street, Tel Aviv. Tel: (023) 65 80 35, Fax: (023) 66 05 58

Italy
Ente Nazionale Germanico per il Turismo, Via Soperga 36, I-20127 Milano. Tel: (02) 26111598, Fax: (02) 2891449 Centro del Turismo Via G Negri 10, I-20123 Milano. Tel: (02) 877323

Japan
German National Tourist Office, Deutsches Kulturzentrum (OAG-Haus), 7-5-56 Akasaka, Minato-ku, Tokyo 107. Tel: (013) 35 86 03 80, Fax: (013) 35 86 50 79

South Africa
German National Tourist Office, c/o Lufthansa German Airlines, 22 Girton Road, Parktown, Johannesburg 2000. Tel: (011) 643 16 15, Fax: (011) 484 27 50

Spain
Oficina Nacional Alemana de Turismo,
San Augustin 2, Plaza de las Cortes,
E-28014 Madrid. Tel: (91) 429 35 51,
Fax: (91) 420 24 50

Sweden
Tyska Turistbyrån, Birger Jarlsgatan 11,
Box 7520, S-10392 Stockholm. Tel: (08)
679 50 95, Fax: (08) 611 11 23

Switzerland
Deutsches Verkehrsbüro, Talstrasse 62,
CH-8001 Zürich. Tel: (01) 221 13 87,
Fax: (01) 212 01 75

United Kingdom
German National Tourist Office, Nightin-
gale House, 65 Curzon Street, London
W1Y 7PE. Tel: (071) 495 39 90, Fax:
(071) 495 61 29

United States
German National Tourist Offices
Los Angeles: 444 South Flower Street,
Suite 2230, Los Angeles CA 90071. Tel:
(213) 688 73 32, Fax: (213) 688 75 74
New York: Chanin Building, 122 East
42nd Street, 52nd floor, New York, N.Y.
10168. Tel: 00 12 12-308 33 00, Fax: 00
12 12-688 13 22
Chicago: c/o German American Chamber
of Commerce, Chicago IL 60603-5978.
Fax: (312) 782 38 91

Tourist Offices in Bavaria

When you're looking for the tourist information centre in a strange town, you
generally ask for the *Fremdenverkehrsamt*,
where you can get general information
(*Auskunft*). In towns designated *Kurort*,
or health resort, the same office is often
called *Kurverwaltung*, spa administration.
As a rule, they're stocked with a full
complement of maps and brochures, many
of them in English; they'll also book hotel rooms in any given price category if
you contact them in advance of your trip.

Munich
Fremdenverkehrsamt, Sendlingerstrasse
1 (Ruffini House), Rindermarkt, 8000
München 2. Tel: 089-23911
also: Hauptbahnhof (opposite Track 11).
Tel: 089-2391256
Landesfremdenverkehrsverband Bayern,
Prinzregentenstrasse 18/IV, Postfach 22
13 52, 8000 München 22. Tel: 089-
212397-0, Fax: 089-293582
**Fremdenverkehrsverband München
Oberbayern**, Sonnenstrasse 10, 8000
München 2. Tel: 089-597347, Fax: 089-
593187

Schwangau (King Ludwig's castles)
Kurverwaltung Schwangau, Münchner
Strasse 2, 8959 Schwangau. Tel: 08362-
81980

Füssen
Kurverwaltung Füssen, Postfach 1165,
8958 Füssen. Tel: 08362-7077

Oberammergau
Verkehrs- und Reisebüro, Gemeinde
Oberammergau, Eugen-Papst-Strasse 9a,
8103 Oberammergau. Tel: 08822-1021

Garmisch-Partenkirchen
Verkehrsamt der Kurverwaltung,
Schnitzschulstrasse 19 , 8100 Garmisch-
Partenkirchen. Tel: 08821-1806

Mittenwald
Kurverwaltung, Dammkarstrasse 3, 8102
Mittenwald. Tel: 08823-33981

Prien/Chiemsee

Kurverwaltung Prien am Chiemsee, Alte Rathausstrasse 10, 8210 Prien am Chiemsee. Tel: 08051-69050

Berchtesgaden

Kurdirektion des Berchtesgadener Landes, Maximilianstrasse 9, 8240 Berchtesgaden. Tel: 08652-5011

Augsburg

Tourist-Information, Bahnhofstrasse 7 (or Rathausplatz), 8900 Augsburg. Tel: 0821-502070
Fremdenverkehrsverband Allgäu/Bayrisch-Schwaben, Fuggerstrasse 9, 8900 Augsburg 1. Tel: 0821-33335, Fax: 0821-38331

Dinkelsbühl

Tourist-Information, Fremdeverkehrsamt, Marktplatz, 8804 Dinkelsbühl. Tel: 09851-90240

Rothenburg ob der Tauber

Kultur- und Fremdenverkehrsamt, Rathaus, 8803 Rothenburg ob der Tauber. Tel: 09861-40492

Würzburg

Fremdenverkehrsamt, Am Congress Centrum, 8700 Würzburg. Tel: 0931-37335 (Offices also located at Haus zum Falken am Markt, Hauptbahnhof.)

Bamberg

Städtisches Fremdenverkehrsamt, Geyerswörthstrasse 3, 8600 Bamberg 12. Tel: 0951-871161

Bayreuth

Gästedienst des Fremdenverkehrsvereins, Luitpoldplatz 9, 8580 Bayreuth. Tel: 0921-88588

Franconian Switzerland

Tourismuszentrale Fränkische Schweiz, Oberes Tor 1, 8553 Ebermannstadt. Tel: 09194-8101

Nuremberg

Congress- und Tourismus-Zentrale Nürnberg, Verkehrsverein Nürnberg, Frauentorgraben 3, 8500 Nürnberg 70. Tel: 0911-23360
(Office also located on Hauptmarkt)
Fremdenverkehrsamt Franken, Postfach 269, Am Plärrer 14, 8500 Nürnberg 81. Tel: 0911-264202, Fax: 0911-270547

Zwiesel

Kurverwaltung, Stadtplatz 27, 8372 Zwiesel. Tel: 09922-1308/9623

Bavarian Forest/Eastern Bavaria

Fremdenverkehrsverband Ostbayern, Landshuterstrasse 13, 8400 Regensburg. Tel: 0941-560260

Regensburg

Tourist-Information Regensburg, Altes Rathaus, 8400 Regensburg. Tel: 0941-507 2141

Passau

Fremdenverkehrsverein Passau, Rathausplatz 3, 8390 Passau. Tel: 0851-33421

Landshut

Verkehrsverein Landshut, Altstadt 315 (Rathaus), 8300 Landshut. Tel: 0871-922050

Consulates

Australia
Godesberger Allee 107, 5300 Bonn 2.
Tel: 0228-81030
Canada
Tal 29, 8000 München. Tel: 089-222661
France
Möhlstrasse 5, 8000 München. Tel: 089-479800/475016
Ireland
Mauerkircherstrasse 1a, 8000 München.
Tel: 089-985723
Italy
Möhlstrasse 3, 8000 München. Tel: 089-4180030
Japan
Prinzregentenplatz 10, 8000 München.
Tel: 089-471043
South Africa
Sendlinger-tor-Platz 5, 8000 München.
Tel: 089-2605081
Spain
Oberföhringerstrasse 45, 8000 München.
Tel: 089-985027
United Kingdom
Bürkleinstrasse 10, 4th floor, 8000
München. Tel: 089-211090
United States
Königinstrasse 5, 8000 München. Tel:
089-28880

FURTHER READING

Insight Guide: Germany (Apa Publications, 1992)
Insight Pocket Guide: Munich (Apa Publications, 1992)
Success by Lion Feuchtwanger (Carrol & Graf)
Rise and Fall of the Third Reich by William Shirer
The History of Germany by Golo Mann (Penguin)
Day Trips in Germany by Earl Steinbicker
Baroque Art in Central Europe (Pelican History of Art)

Index

INSIGHT GUIDES

COLORSET NUMBERS

You'll find the colorset number on the spine of each Insight Guide.